The Art of Islamic Lawmaking

Bahiya Najwa

Table of Contents

ABSTRACT 1

RÉSUMÉ 1

ACKNOWLEDGEMENTS 2

INTRODUCTION 4

CHAPTER ONE 9

   Sharia and *Fiqh* 9

   Conclusion 31

CHAPTER TWO 32

   Premise One of the Dominant Historiography 35

   Anti-Orientalist Variations and Refinements 44

   Criminal Law According to *fiqh* 52

   Evidence and Procedure According to *fiqh* 54

   Conclusion 61

CHAPTER THREE 64

   Religious and Political Authority in Early Islamic History 65

   Siyāsa 68

   Premise Two of the Dominant Historiography 72

   The Problem of Defining What the Sharia is 77

CHAPTER FOUR 108

Conclusion 108

ABSTRACT

This thesis attempts to challenge the dominant historiography in the field of Islamic law and expand our understanding to show that it is more than just the *fiqh* of jurists. Jurists' law, characterized as a sacred law, arguably reached its final form in the 10th Century CE as an ideal unchanging theory that is the yardstick for the application of Islamic law. Due to this alleged inability to change and its rigidity, Islamic law failed to accommodate the needs of society and proved impractical for governance and ruling authorities created their own secular legal system. This thesis attempts to overcome the dichotomy of a "sacred" and a "secular" law and instead takes into account the practice of the state, its agents, and the laity as equally legitimate and competing manifestations in the overall discourse of Islamic law. As a result, the law never ceased to evolve, but rather, the subject matter and the institutions of Islamic law kept changing over time. Therefore, Islamic law should be understood as a process where the different actors continue to shape and reshape the "correct" form, content, and application thereof.

INTRODUCTION

The dominant contemporary approach to understanding how Islamic law was constructed historically describes something, according to legal history professor Amr Shalakany, like the creation of a "plot": a narrative about the history, development, and subsequent decline of Islamic law that is pre-determined by earlier scholars, and which creates the framework for further research.[1] The founders of Islamic legal studies in the West, Joseph Schacht and Noel Coulson, established such a narrative by relying on "a certain set of primary materials," by including "certain key actors and events," while excluding "others outside its narrative.[2] Recent scholars like Wael Hallaq, Mohammad Fadel, Sherman Jackson and others have attempted to challenge this approach. But although their work has made significant modifications and refinements to the theories presented by Schacht and Coulson, others have claimed that they did not challenge the earlier premises and instead confined themselves to the original framework.

According to Schacht, Islamic law is a jurists' law developed by religious scholars, as reflected in the *fiqh* literature.[3] He also argues that due to its failure of accommodating the continuously changing demands of the society, Islamic law had to yield to custom and the practice of political authorities.[4] Therefore, Schacht (and others, such as Coulson) held the opinion that because of the rigidity and the religious character of Islamic law, it did not lend itself to practical governance in a dynamic society, which according to them opened a gap between theory and practice. The outcome was that the ideal Islamic law, created by Muslim jurists, was replaced by secular laws created by the ruler and his agents. Here we

---

[1] Amr. A. Shalakany, "Islamic Legal Histories," *Berkeley Journal of Middle Eastern & Islamic Law* 1 (2008): p. 3-5.

[2] Ibid, p. 3, where it writes verbatim:" I argue the story of Islamic-law-past has also been woven around a certain 'plot,' one that relies on a certain set of primary materials, features certain key actors and events, leaves others outside its narrative, and thus implicitly subscribes to a number of foundational premises to define what counts as 'Islamic' and what passes for 'law' in the historian's tale."

[3] Joseph Schacht, *An Introduction to Islamic Law* (Oxford: Clarendon Press, 1964), p. 5.

[4] Schacht, *An Introduction to Islamic Law*, p. 76-77.

see a clear distinction between legal theory, legal discourse and the practice of the state. According to this narrative, Muslim societies were deprived of a legal system that could have been able to respond effectively to the interests of their societies. Since they regard Islamic law as a religious law, in the sense that it is understood as unchanging and eternal, it did not develop in connection with the practice of the community and the state. Instead Islamic law preceded them.[5] By looking at several examples from the Mamluk and Ottoman periods found in recent scholarship this thesis seeks to cast doubt on the dominant narrative of lawmaking in Islam. We should not restrict ourselves to the legal discourse of jurists attempting to understand law disconnected from its interaction with a certain reality, legal practice. Instead, we should consider further actors along with jurists in the overall discourse of Islamic law, such as the state, its agents, and non-jurists in general. This means that each actors' conception of the law and interaction with the law contributes to the evolution of Islamic law, whether he or she is reaching his conception of the law through deriving rulings through a legal theory from legal indicants found in scripture or by intending to satisfy the 'aims found in the divine sources, or by supplementing the law through customary law and *siyāsa* measures that at least do not contradict the spirit of the Sharia, or judges and other agents of the state who use their discretion in favor of the spirit and at the expense of the letter of the law, or even the common people who cause legal experts and judges to find solutions for brand new legal problems or new constellations of older legal cases.

In the last few decades we can observe the appearance of a new body of secondary literature that attempts to break out of this framework and introduce a new approach to the understanding of lawmaking in Islam. This has happened primarily through the integration

---

[5] Mohammed Fadel, "State and the Sharia," in *The Ashgate Research Companion to Islamic Law*, ed. Rudolph Peters et al. (Surrey: Ashgate Publishing Press, 2014), p. 95.

of two things: Islamic legal practice and the role of the state. This thesis attempts to take these new approaches and integrate them into a broader understanding of Islamic law. The study will also demonstrate the implications of the dominant historiography of Islamic law, namely that "a lot of what your average American post-realist lawyer would take for legal history happens to fall outside the dominant plot of Islamic law historiography."[6] This would include among others commercial customs, administrative rules of Abbasid bureaucracy, criminal justice measures of the Mamluk rulers, or the structures of Ottoman political governance.[7]

Ultimately this thesis seeks to prove the validity of this new approach and show that Islamic law should not simply be seen as a collection of substantive rulings, but rather as a comprehensive system of legal thought where several actors are participants in a continuous process of negotiation over the correct expression of the law. In this respect, jurists, judges, the state and even the laity played a larger or smaller role in the development of the law. This process, however, was not always one of harmony, but often times characterized by conflicting claims over the legitimate scope and function in the legal sphere. This new understanding would have wide-reaching consequences, when it comes to issues of legal reform and how both Muslims and Western observers approach the *sharī'ah* (Islamic law).

The selection of the term "lawmaking" is intentional, and denotes a wider understanding of Islamic law, its actors and its sources while avoiding controversial and unclearly defined terms such as "legal methodology" or "legal philosophy." Under "lawmaking" we will subsume everything that influences the legal outcome. Islamic law comprises several literary genres and academic disciplines such as *furū' al-fiqh*, which

---

[6] Shalakany, "Islamic Legal Histories," p. 6.
[7] Ibid. p. 6.

outlines the substantive body of norms, and *uṣūl al-fiqh*, which deals with the identification

and classification of the sources of the law and the process of deriving rules from these

sources. In principle, the latter puts forward a legal methodology from which the jurist can

deduct legal norms that are expounded in the former. Besides those two very important

genres and academic disciplines there are several others that are related to them, as for

example *qawā ʿid al-fiqhiyyah* (legal maxims) and *maqāṣid al-sharī ʿa*, which can be

rendered as the intentions of the law. Together, these texts combine to elucidate a larger

process of "lawmaking" that goes beyond basic understanding of texts of substantive law.

What we talked about so far is part and parcel of the *fiqh*-discourse of jurists and herein

lies the main focus of the dominant historiography in their study of Islamic law. This

picture gets further complicated by adding the concept of *siyāsa* and notions of public

welfare (*maṣlaḥa*) into our discussion.[8]

---

[8] That Islamic law is more than *fiqh* is argued by Kristen Stilt:" Islamic law does not exist on its own as a set of rules set forth by God. Even after doctrine has been articulated by jurists, that law is not itself an actor: humans, such as the judge, *muhtasib*, mufti, sultan, and Muslims generally give it meaning at the social level." Kristen Stilt, *Islamic Law in Action: Authority, Discretion, and Everyday Experiences in Mamluk Egypt* (New York: Oxford University Press, 2012), p. 10. See further: In her study Leslie Peirce talks about "a culture in which normative law responded to the messy complexity of real life", where "the judge considered each case on its individual merits but in reference to normative law, and individuals strategized by drawing on local knowledge of the meaning and mechanics of legal rules and processes." Ibid., p. 5 (Citing p. 111, from Peirce, Leslie. *Morality Tales: Law and Gender in the Ottoman Court of Aintab*. Berkeley: University of California Press, 2003); Based on his study Boğaç Ergene concludes that "the court records attribute a rule-oriented character to judicial processes" while at the same time the courts "had the ability to appropriate more socially conciliatory modes of dispute management, when this was deemed necessary. This flexibility is consistent with my claim in this book that the Ottoman courts were responsive to social, political, and cultural pressures in their localities." Ibid., p. 5 (Citing p. 211, from Ergene, Boğaç. *Local Court, Provincial Society, and Justice in the Ottoman Empire: Legal Practice and Dispute Resolution in Çankırı and Kastamonu (1652-1744)*. Leiden: Brill, 2003); David Powers demonstrates how extra-legal considerations had an impact on the *muftīs* opinion-making, so that their responses could be seen as the "product of combined legal and extra-legal factors." Ibid., p. 5 (Citing p. 232, from Powers, David. *Law, Society, and Culture in the Maghrib, 1300-1500*. Cambridge: Cambridge University Press, 2002); Judith Tucker argues that both the *muftis*, producing the *fatāwā*, and the courts, applying them "did not eschew the Islamic legal doctrines they had inherited, which viewed male-female difference as a fundamental reality of social life," but they "seemed to opt, whenever possible, for the broader and more flexible interpretation of the law, for the interpretation that appeared to best serve the interests of justice as well as the needs and stability of their community." "This was all done under the heading of the applicable law, which offered, in addition to 'certain incontrovertible principles and rules,' the possibility of an outcome that promoted community harmony through a selection of textual sources and of variable interpretations." Ibid., p. 6 (Citing p. 181-182, from Tucker, Judith. *In the House of the Law: Gender and Islamic Law in Ottoman Syria and Palestine*. Berkeley: University of California Press, 1988).

Importance of the Research

Popular notions of Islamic law are partly informed by the dominant historiography, which tells us that Islamic law is a fixed sacred code in contradiction with (Western) modernity, human rights, and democracy. Today we also find large Muslim communities in North America and Europe as well as vast refugee movements from the Middle East into the West, being met with concerns about a perceived "Islamization". This fear is partly based on prevalent notions about Islamic law and the idea that, through an influx of Muslim refugees, Western societies would be affected in negative ways. A new understanding of what is meant by "Islamic law," informed by recent scholarly approaches, would help to challenge this belief. Third, a critical reevaluation of the history of Islamic law can play a crucial role in the reform of Islamic law today, as the notion that Islamic law is unchanging and fixed is also quite prevalent among Muslims themselves. Muslims may be more inclined to consider rulings that differ from the traditional rulings found in popular *fiqh* works by famous scholars of the past if they would see how those rulings were applied in practice.

Outline

The thesis comprises five chapters, with the first being the Introduction. The next chapter (Chapter One) will lay out basic notions and concepts concerning the Sharia, which will feature a short survey of what has been said in this regard by some famous Western scholars of Islamic law. Further, this chapter will try to highlight a few similarities and overlaps between Western legal systems and the Sharia as a legal system.

Chapter Two then will explore the dominant historiography of lawmaking in Islam with its underlying premises and assumptions, followed by a selected set of responses that challenges some very fundamental conclusions of the dominant historiography, particularly regarding the question of whether change after the supposed "closure of the gate of *ijtihād*" was possible or not. The second half of the third chapter will focus on Criminal law and rules on evidence and procedure as found in *fiqh*-works.

Chapter Three will outline the new approaches and show how these new conceptions differ from the dominant approach, as well as explain how these new insights arose. In this chapter, we will also look at legal practice and discuss the role of the state, of his agents and other non-legal factors in the lawmaking process, which will cast doubt on the dominant historiography's narrative of Islamic law and at the same time put forward an argument for a broader conception of Sharia. In that regard we will pick up the discussion of Criminal law and rules on evidence and procedure found in Chapter Two, but now going beyond of what is written in works of *fiqh*. Finally, Chapter Four will be the conclusion.

The transcription of Arabic terms and names will follow the transliteration system as proposed in the journal *Islamic Law and Society* (ILS). Year dates will be aimed at the Julien- and Gregorian calendar expressing the year in Common Era (CE). Names of cities and Arabic terms that made their way into the English language such as Sharia, Koran, Sunna, and Muhammad are written in their anglicized form and will not be transliterated. The content of this paper is restricted to the premodern period of Islam and will focus on the Sunni stream of Islam. Unfortunately, the scope of the paper does not allow to include Shiite or Ibadi discourses.

CHAPTER ONE

<u>Sharia and *Fiqh*</u>

The term Sharia is a multifaceted term. It can have a very comprehensive meaning in the sense of Islamic "normativity in the fields of ritual, morality and law". In this regard the term "Islamic law" would be used in the same way like Jewish law is. In a more specific and narrow sense one can use the term "Islamic law" as just referring to the "legal normativity of the sharia".[9]

In the standard works of Islamic jurisprudence "Sharia" is defined as the sum of divine injunctions (*ahkām,* sg. *hukm*) that were "revealed to humanity through God's messenger Muhammad." As such they are to be found in the Koran and the divinely inspired sayings and behavior of the prophet, called Sunna. The Sunna is accessed through the *hadīth* collections. Those two sets of texts should not be confused with law-codes. They embody the raw material for lawmaking in Islam from which through the application of interpretation and reasoning rules are derived. This is a human endeavor that is called *fiqh* (jurisprudence). The term *fiqh* is also used for the result of this process, the substantive rulings (*furū'*) that are to be found in the works of jurists (*fāqih,* pl. *fuqahā'*). It is also not uncommon to see that the terms Sharia and *fiqh* are used interchangeably.[10] In sum we could say:

> "...the Sharia is the set of divine commands, transmitted by God through the foundational sources of Quran and Sunna, and fiqh is the human endeavor to identify and elucidate these divine injunctions."[11]

So, we assume a conceptual difference between the Sharia as the perfect law in the mind of God, and *fiqh* as the human endeavor to understand the Sharia.[12] Accordingly, *fiqh* as a human project, can only be a probable approximation of the divine Sharia, in the sense

---

[9] Rudolph Peters and Peri Bearman, "Introduction: The Nature of the Sharia," in *The Ashgate Research Companion to Islamic Law*, ed. Rudolph Peters et al. (Surrey: Ashgate Publishing Press, 2014), p. 1.

[10] Ibid.

[11] Ibid.

[12] Anver M. Emon, "To Most Likely Know the Law: Objectivity and Authority, and Interpretation in Islamic Law," *Hebraic Political Studies* 4 (2009): p. 418.

of the law in the mind of God, and there is no "book" that contains "the Sharia".[13] Instead we have to turn to the writings of jurists.

If somebody was to read those texts, he or she will recognize a number of divergent and contradicting views present in them. Usually those views are presented next to each other and the author does not aim to resolve the contradictions. Thomas Bauer tells us that this is not to be seen as a failure to do so, but instead, it was not intended to resolve them to begin with. There seem to be societies in which it is possible for more or less irreconcilable norms and values to exist next to each other, without insisting on the sole legitimacy of only one of them. People living in such societies do not seek indisputable truths, but are rather content with looking for probabilities, which leads to the deliberate production of ambiguities.[14]

The Road to Ambiguity

However, the reader has to be aware that this status quo Bauer is talking about was the result of a historical process. In the early history of Islam there were attempts to opt for a uniform legal system in the form of a code, in order to provide more legal certainty. Ibn Muqaffaʿ (d. 756 CE), for example, who was a courtier of the Abbasid caliph al-Manṣūr (d. 754 CE), urged the caliph to create a legal code, because of the existence of contradictory laws among different parts, and even inside the same cities of the empire. This project was opposed by the jurists and was not put into practice.[15] An ambiguous system was favored by jurists, because a uniform *fiqh* was impossible to achieve due to the linguistic ambiguity

---

[13] Bauer, Die Kultur der Ambiguität, p. 158.

[14] Thomas Bauer, *Die Kultur der Ambiguität: Eine andere Geschichte des Islam* (Berlin: Verlag Der Weltreligionen, 2011), p.12-13. See further Zysow, Aron. *The Economy of Certainty: An Introduction to the Typology of Islamic Legal Theory.* Atlanta: Lockwood Press, 2013.

[15] Shelomo D. Goitein, *Studies in Islamic History and Institutions* (Leiden: Brill, 2010), p. 162; Ahmed Fekry Ibrahim, *Pragmatism in Islamic law: A Social and Intellectual History* (Syracuse: Syracuse University Press, 2015), p. 35-36.

in the sources and the flexible hermeneutic of the jurists.[16] Another Abbasid caliph, al-Ma'mūn (d. 833 CE), tried to impose his will on the jurists through the so called *miḥna*, the Koranic inquisition that lasted from 833 CE to 849 CE. The religious scholars (*'ālim,* pl. *'ulamā'*) emerged victorious against the caliph, resulting in a so called "constitutional arrangement", according to which from that point onwards only jurists had the prerogative to develop the law, whereas the state's role in the legal sphere was reduced to the enforcement and execution of the jurists' law.[17]

When talking about this phenomenon in his book, Bauer draws on the concept *Ambiguitätstoleranz* (ambiguity tolerance-intolerance) that is borrowed from psychology. Communities in various cultures and epochs differ starkly in their sensibilities towards ambiguities, vagueness, diversity and pluralism, and in the way, they dealt with them. At times and places people tried to get rid of them and aimed to create a world of unambiguity and absolute truths, while others merely sought to restrain ambiguity. In the case of the pre-modern Islamic world we can say that the dominant trend was to reduce ambiguity only to a manageable degree and tame it, in order to be able to live with it, but the aim was never to get rid of it.[18]

In that sense, we could understand the canonization of the Koran and *ḥadīth* or efforts to increase predictability of the law as such a process of reducing ambiguity in pre-

---

[16] Matthias Rohe, *Islamic Law in Past and Present,* trans. Gwendolin Goldbloom (Leiden: Brill, 2014), p. 14; Ibrahim, *Pragmatism in Islamic law,* p. 35; Regarding the "mutual toleration" of the four Sunni schools see p. 67 in Schacht, *An Introduction to Islamic Law*; Furthermore, not every tradition privileged probability over certainty in law. The *ẓāhirī* school for example required every law to be certain. Aron Zysow, *The Economy of Certainty: An Introduction to the Typology of Islamic Legal Theory* (Atlanta: Lockwood Press, 2013), p. 3.

[17] Ibrahim, *Pragmatism in Islamic law,* p. 36; Knut Vikør, *Between God and the Sultan: A History of Islamic Law* (London: Hurst & Company, 2005), p. 95. However, was there really such a strict division of labor in the sense that the ruler was not allowed to interfere in the jurists' endeavor of "creating" the law, and thereby everyone other than jurists was denied the right to decide what the Sharia is? (More on this in chapter Three).

[18] Bauer, *Die Kultur der Ambiguität,* p.13. However, starting in the modern period and today one can observe a gradual shift from a former high tolerance of ambiguity towards intolerance of ambiguity. The process of modernization in Islamic cultures seems to be a process of eliminating ambiguity. While scholars of the 14th century perceived the existence of several possible readings of the Koran (*qirā'a)* as a source of richness, contemporary Muslims often view this as a nuisance (p.15). The same can be said concerning an array of topics, such as the interpretation of the Koran (*tafsīr*), the difference of opinion among legal scholars (*ikhtilāf*), etc.

modern Islamic societies. Furthermore, it is possible to argue that processes aimed to reduce ambiguity were triggered by a crisis in the form of an ambiguity-surplus.[19] This was also the case with the redaction of the Koran and the designation of specific *ḥadīth* - collections[20] as authoritative, both of which represent the fundament and starting point for Islamic legal thought.[21]

Where to find God's Law?

Scholars sought to create a law that is in accordance with God's will and not based on pure human legislation. Revelation was the only means to know the divine will. With the death of the prophet revelation came to an end and scholars were left with a limited amount of "God's speech" which comprised an even smaller amount of unambiguous sections, and yet an even smaller number of verses that could be regarded as relevant for legal matters.[22]

In that regard is very important to understand the epistemology of Muslim scholars, who draw a substantial distinction in their assessment of the trustworthiness of knowledge and its quality in acting as a proof, which they applied to both Koran and *ḥadīth*. The former relates to the way knowledge or information is transmitted and received (*riwāya*), whereby the latter refers to the explicitness of the content of a piece of knowledge or information *(dalāla)*. Both can be either deemed certain *(qaṭ ʿī)* or uncertain *(ẓannī)*. In terms of *ḥadīth* this means that if a specific report is narrated through a particular number

---

[19] Ibid., p. 57.

[20] Also, called *al-kutub al-sitta,* among which the two collections Ṣaḥīḥ al-Bukhārī and Ṣaḥīḥ al-Muslim hold a special status and are referred to as *ṣaḥīḥān.*

[21] Bauer, *Die Kultur der Ambiguität*, p. 145-147. A crisis in the form of the death of several people who memorized the Koran, triggered the redaction of the Koran. This can be seen as a first instance of restricting pluralism, in order to create a canon, a standard authoritative text of the Koran. The creation of a *ḥadīth* canon serves as a second example of restricting pluralism. For this look at Brown, Jonathan. *The Canonization of al-Bukhārī and Muslim: The Formation and Function of the Sunni Ḥadīth Canon.* Leiden: Brill, 2007.

[22] Umar F. Abd-Allah, "Theological Dimensions of Islamic Law," in *The Cambridge Companion to Classical Islamic Theology*, ed. Tim Winter. (Cambridge: Cambridge University Press, 2008), p. 239.

of independent and uninterrupted chains of transmission *(isnād)*, where every narrator

(rāwī) is to be known as a trustworthy person, who could have actually met each other,

then this report is certain in its transmission and is called *khabar mutawātir*. There are only

a few number of reports, which fall into this category. The remainder, which makes up the

majority of reports, including the bulk of the two *ṣaḥīḥān* collections of al-Bukhārī (d. 869

CE) and Muslim (d. 874 CE), fall into the category that does not meet the aforementioned

stringent conditions and are therefore uncertain in their transmission *(khabar wāhid)*.

Prophetic reports that fall into this category are then further divided into several sub-

categories such as for example *ṣaḥīḥ*, *ḥasan* and *ḍa ʿīf*.[23]

The way of transmission of the Koranic text on the other hand is regarded to be

certain in its entirety. However, even if it is established that a piece of knowledge or

information is certain in its transmission, it does not mean that the content itself and what

one can understand from it is certain as well. This is true for both, the Koran and the

khabar mutawātir. If for example the wording of a text is very clear and only allows for

one definite meaning and interpretation, then it is certain and unambiguous in its meaning

(dalāla). But if the text is ambiguous and therefore allows for more than one interpretation,

then it is uncertain in its meaning, independent of the fact that this text is certain in its

transmission.[24] In the case of *ḥadīth*, scholars did not claim whether a report is true or

false, but instead they were concerned with degrees of certainty, which would decide for

what kind of purposes a *ḥadīth* could be used.[25] This concept of epistemology is one of the

main factors that allows for the pluralism of opinion that is inherent to Islamic law and is

key to be aware of when reading juristic works. Additionally, the above mentioned

---

[23] Wahba Zuḥaylī, *Al-Wajīz fī Uṣūl al-Fiqh* (Dimashq: Dār al-Fikr, 1994), p. 25, 32. and p. 36-37.
[24] Ibid., p. 24-25 and p. 32-33, and p. 37.
[25] Bauer, Die Kultur der Ambiguität, p. 156.

"constitutional arrangement" showed that the independent community of jurists efficiently opposed the state's attempt to impose any kind of legal code. (More on this below in chapter Three).

Natures of the Sharia

The above-mentioned comprehensiveness of Sharia seems to be a very distinct sort of law in contrast to common-law or civil-law traditions. Nevertheless, there seem to be a number of commonalities between those legal systems, more than what a lay man could imagine. If we want to look at those common features and processes, we have to turn our attention towards the strictly legal elements of the Sharia, as opposed to its religious and moral elements. What I mean by strictly legal elements are those rules of the Sharia whose compliance "can be enforced by the judiciary or by the executive state organs." If it cannot be enforced, then that rule does not fall under the category of "legal", but rather under the category of "religious" or "moral", in which case non-compliance would not entail any worldly legal consequences, but maybe consequences in the hereafter, as a matter between a person and God, without a third party being involved.[26]

This kind of distinction between various contours of the Sharia is also reflected in the separation of norms done by Muslim jurists, who distinguished between rules of worship ('ibādāt) and rules of social conduct, or civil obligations (mu'āmalāt). Additionally, they further divided rules between the domain of adjudication (qaḍā'), which includes rules that are enforceable in this world, and the domain of conscience (diyāna), which in contrast includes rules that are not enforceable in this world, and only affect the relationship between the believer and God. It is important to point out that those

---

[26] Peters and Bearman, "Introduction: The Nature of the Sharia," p. 1-2.

boundaries are not always clear cut and sometimes overlap.[27]

Now we will have a closer look at the main "natures" of the Sharia and how they differ from each other. In doing so, we will look at the Sharia's non-legal elements, which are not enforceable, and at its strictly legal elements that are enforceable. We attempt to demarcate those layers, but this does not mean that we view them as mutually exclusive or contradicting each other. Even though, in the following we will look at the Sharia under separate headings, it is very important to point out that obedience to the Sharia as a whole is a moral obligation for Muslims, even if the legal element dominates or is completely absent. Regardless of enforceability, for Muslims the whole of the law is religious.

However, keeping this caveat in mind, we will present those layers separate, because we intend to point out how some Western scholars conceptualized the Sharia, which at times reduced the Sharia to only one of the mentioned elements.

Non-Legal Elements of the Sharia

Sharia as Religious Law

Primarily one could characterize the Sharia as a religious law, because Muslims believe it to be a law revealed by God, through his prophet. Thus, the believer should abide by it if he seeks salvation in the afterlife. Furthermore, we can identify a number of rules that fall in the category of rituals and worship (*'ibādāt*), which are mainly "meaningful in the relationship between a believer and his or her creator." A glance into the opening chapters of a legal manual (*fiqh* book) suffices to notice that. One will see that those chapters revolve around the famous 'five pillars of Islam' and everything that is relevant to them, such as rulings pertaining to ritual purity (*ṭahāra*), ritual prayer (*ṣalāt*), fasting during the month of Ramadān (*ṣawm*), religious alms tax (*zakāt*), and performing the pilgrimage to

---

[27] Ibid.

Mecca (*ḥajj*). Aside from rulings concerning the five pillars of Islam, there are several other chapters in legal manuals (*fiqh* books) that deal with primarily 'religious' instructions. Among those we find chapters on what kinds of food and beverages are allowed for consumption (*ḥalāl, dhabīḥa*), circumcision, whether music is permissible or not, wearing jewelry, which parts of the body are allowed to be visible in public (*'awra*), ways of salutation, accepting dinner invitations etc.[28]

Religious Law from a Western Point of View

Western historiography discussed the religious character of the Sharia and often times used that element to identify it as the only mainstay of the Sharia, which at a first glance does not seem problematic, because Muslims themselves conceive of their law as religious.

The problem was however, that when some Western scholars characterized the Sharia solely as a religious law, they assumed that the Sharia is irrational and unadaptable in contrast to Western non-religious legal systems, because of its religious character. Among one of the main proponents of that view was the famous German sociologist Max Weber (d. 1920), who played an important role in making this position acceptable in academia. His point of departure was to compare religion based legal systems (Islam, Judaism) with Roman law. In Roman law, he saw the highest degree of legal rationality and regarded it as the foundation of most Western legal systems. Weber argued that religious lawmaking as opposed to rational decision-making is rooted in revelation and therefore cannot be rational. Moreover, religious laws would include non-legal considerations, such as magic or supernatural elements in their adjudication. Since the Sharia is the law of the religion of Islam – a religious law – this reasoning must be true for

---

[28] Ibid.

Islam as well, according to Weber. And, because the Sharia is derived from fixed revealed texts, he further characterized it as rigid and unadaptable.[29] The motive of Islamic law being rigid was borrowed by Weber from Christiaan Snouck Hurgronje (d. 1936), who was a Dutch colonial official and scholar. According to him *fiqh* was a very unrealistic, impractical and purely theoretical construct.[30]

The notions and ideas of Weber in regard to Islamic law where echoed and reiterated by several scholars following him. This went so far that those characterizations of the Sharia became the dominant view in Western historiography up until the 1970's, although this kind of scholarship was not based on "any empirical research into sharia practice." Those views only started to be seriously questioned, when scholars focused their research towards the study of court records, "Islamic law in action".[31]

As we have seen, the argument is that Islamic law is rigid and unadaptable because it is a religious law. Even further, it is supposed to be "an all-embracing body of religious duties, the totality of Allah's command that regulate the life of every Muslim in all its aspects."[32] Bauer rightfully points out that the characterization of Islamic law as a religious or divine law is misleading in the sense that it absolutizes the religious aspect of the law and by doing so creating the impression that there is no "secular" element in the law.[33] As aforementioned, legal manuals contain several chapters dealing with "religious" instructions. However, when we look into legal manuals we will see that the area of worship does not even make up half of the topics of the overall content. Taking Abū Isḥāq

---

[29] Ibid., p. 2-3. For more on Weber and Islamic law see Ibrahim, Ahmed Fekry. "Rethinking the *Taqlīd* Hegemony: An Institutional, *Longue-Durée* Approach." 2016.

[30] Ibid., p. 2-3. See also Joseph Schacht:" Islamic law is a particularly instructive example of a 'sacred law'. It is a phenomenon so different from all other forms of law." In Schacht, *An introduction to Islamic Law*, p.1-2.

[31] Ibid., p. 3. See also Johansen, Baber. *Contingency in a Sacred Law: Legal and Ethical Norms in the Muslim Fiqh*. Leiden: Brill, 1999, p. 46-54.

[32] Schacht, An Introduction to Islamic Law, p.1-2.

[33] Bauer, Die Kultur der Ambiguität, p.157.

al-Shirāzī's (d. 1083 CE) work of *shāfi 'ī fiqh* as an example, Bauer shows that chapters on worship in terms of actual content constitute roughly one-third of the book. And, those chapters only deal with acts of worship and are not concerned with questions of speculative theology (*kalām*) or Sufism (*taṣawwuf*). They do not cover all questions of the religion. In that sense, Bauer compares treatises of *fiqh* with Roman Law, which also covered topics of ritual.[34]

Chapters on administrative law are completely absent, while criminal law, constitutional law and military law are the least developed areas of law found in Islamic legal manuals.[35] So we cannot speak of an all-embracing body of law.

Contrary to that there are only a limited number of fields fixed by more or less explicit texts, as for instance family law, inheritance law, Koranic penal punishments, and law on foundations and trusts.[36] One could say that the law is silent on an array of topics.

In response to scholars such as Hurgronje who saw *fiqh* as a theoretical construct without practical relevance, Rohe cites recent scholars who have shown that Islamic law was in fact relevant for the practiced law. Depending on the field it is possible to see substantial correspondence between theory and practice, as is the case in personal status or inheritance law.[37]

Sharia as Moral Law

In addition to acts of worship and enforceable rules, the Sharia also comprises a set of ordinances that can be understood as ethics or moral qualifications of acts. This constitutes such a huge chunk of the Sharia that several Western scholars went as far as to deny the

---

[34] Thomas Bauer, "Normative Ambiguitätstoleranz im Islam," in *Gewohnheit. Gebot. Gesetz. Normativität in Geschichte und Gegenwart: eine Einführung*, ed. Nils Jansen et al. (Tübingen: Mohr Siebeck, 2011), p. 157-158.
[35] Ibid., p. 159.
[36] Matthias Rohe, *Islamic Law in Past and Present*, trans. Gwendolin Goldbloom (Brill, 2014), p. 17.
[37] Ibid., p. 98.

legal character of the Sharia. For example, the aforementioned Dutch scholar Hurgronje instead characterized the Sharia as a "deontology", a system comprised of moral obligations. Kevin Reinhart prefers the term "morality" over "law", when translating the word Sharia, because such a rendering would underline the fact that the Sharia serves as the fundamental moral basis for the Muslim community.[38]

The legal philosopher H.L.A Hart (d. 1992) said that "…it is in no sense a necessary truth that laws reproduce or satisfy certain demands of morality,"[39] which also means that law does not have to mirror the views, demands and pressures of the society. Contrary to a secularist or positivist conception of law, in the case of Islam, law and morality are derived from the same divine sources. Thus, this assumption of the Sharia's conflation of morality with law was another subject to criticism by Western scholars.[40] Noel Coulson for example describes the Sharia in the following terms:

> "a rigid and immutable system, embodying norms of an absolute and eternal validity, which are not susceptible to modification by any legislative authority"[41]

He attributes this alleged 'rigidity' of the law to the connection of morality and law as found in the Sharia.[42] However, there are also Western scholars who are not so critical of this conflation of law and morality, but rather saw that connection as something very positive. In that regard they argued that it would enhance the law's efficacy. When for example acts of worship and the fulfilling of and adhering to mundane matters are both part of a divine normative system with its repercussions for the afterlife, then a believer

---

[38] Peters and Bearman, "Introduction: The Nature of the Sharia," p. 3.
[39] Ibid., p. 3; H.L.A. Hart, *The Concept of Law* (Oxford: Clarendon Press, 1994), p. 184-185.
[40] Peters and Bearman, "Introduction: The Nature of the Sharia," p. 3.
[41] Noel J. Coulson, *A History of Islamic Law* (Edinburgh: Edinburgh University Press, 1978), p. 5.
[42] Peters and Bearman, "Introduction: The Nature of the Sharia," p. 3.

would supposedly be more eager to abide by the law in all kinds of affairs.[43] One famous scholar who holds such an opinion is Wael Hallaq, who argues that this intimate connection between morality and law equipped the law:

> "with efficient, communally based, socially embedded, bottom-top methods of control that rendered it remarkably efficient in commanding willing obedience and – as [another] consequence – [made it] less coercive than any imperial law Europe had known since the fall of the Roman Empire."[44]

Moreover, if we look at debates of Western legal philosophers on the relationship between law and morality, we can see that the sharp contrast between the Sharia and Western legal systems on that question is misleading. Even though European philosophers distinguished between man-made law and morality, they discussed the link between the two in the light of (against the backdrop of) which criteria one has to follow in order to create good laws.[45]

As for example Thomas Aquinas (d. 1274) and other advocates of natural law, who conceived of an ideal type of law that rests on reason and morality. As being part of the natural order, such a law would also have to be consistent with the objectives of nature. They held the view that therefore man-made law has to conform to that natural law, of which morality is a part of, and only then law could be regarded as valid and binding. In contrast to that position stand those who do not require the law to be in conformity with morality. This position was put forward by legal positivists such as John Austin (d. 1859). According to their view the relationship between law and morality is only loose and any overlap between the two is merely accidental. Hart on the other side required that law and

---

[43] Ibid.

[44] Wael B. Hallaq, *Sharīʿa: Theory, Practice, Transformations* (Cambridge: Cambridge University Press, 2009), p. 2.

[45] Peters and Bearman, "Introduction: The Nature of the Sharia," p. 4.

morality have to be in line with each other, since the two deal with the same issues

regarding human behavior and central human values.[46]

When we turn to the standard *fiqh* works, we can observe that jurists did not present

moral and legal rules separate from each other. Nevertheless, as mentioned before, rules in

fiqh works are qualified as belonging to one of the two, the domain of adjudication (legal

rules, *qaḍā'*) or the domain of conscience (moral rules, *diyāna*). According to both Muslim

scholars and the criteria of present-day (Western) philosophy the majority of Sharia rules

(as found in *fiqh* works!) are moral, as opposed to being strictly legal.[47]

Sharia as "the Law"

Now we will move on to talk about the purely legal aspects of the Sharia, which comprises

its "enforceable legal norms dealing with obligations and rights between humans".[48] With

purely legal aspects I refer to those elements and concepts that characterize a legal system

and are shared by the Sharia and Western legal systems, as nicely expressed in the

following quote:

> "If law is a binding custom or practice of a community, requiring people to perform or
>
> abstain from certain actions, and if law is a system that resolves conflicts and makes
>
> rules, applies, and enforces them, then the Sharia is as much a law and legal system as
>
> the next one."[49]

As such Peters and Bearman describe the Sharia with attributes like positivist,

---

[46] Ibid., p. 4; See for a short overview of different conceptions of law in Western legal traditions look at p. 91-96 in
Lundmark, Thomas. *Charting the Divide between Common and Civil law*. Oxford: Oxford University Press, 2012.

[47] Peters and Bearman, "Introduction: The Nature of the Sharia," p. 4. In regards to present-day (Western) philosophy, rules
count as moral, in so far as they fulfill the following formal criteria: "(1) moral rules address significant issues (such as
those related to human life, property, sexuality); (2) they cannot or can hardly be changed deliberately…; (3) they only
judge voluntary behavior; and (4) they are only complied with by virtue of individual conscience and social pressure,
not by force." In Peters and Bearman, "Introduction: The Nature of the Sharia," p. 4.

[48] Ibid., p. 5.

[49] Ibid.

pragmatic and dynamic. Furthermore, the difference between the religious and moral

Sharia on the one side and the legal Sharia on the other side is that while the former plays

in a context where compliance is mainly up to the conscience of a person, this is not true

for the latter. Legal rules were not up to the conscience of the people, but rather they were

enforced through state institutions like the judiciary and the executive. In that regard the

interaction between Sharia and *siyāsa* is of crucial importance[50], a topic that will be subject

to a more in-depth discussion in chapter Three.

This is also supported by the fact that whereas religious and moral aspects of the

Sharia only address the Muslim believer, the Sharia as law applies to all subjects living

under its jurisdiction, to Muslims and non-Muslims alike. For example, even though, the

different Christian and Jewish communities had their own religious courts regulating

family law, Rossita Gradeva shows that Christians in Ottoman Bulgaria actively made use

of the *qāḍī* courts for different reasons, even in matters of family law. Those cases involve

Christian women that preferred to bring their case in front of a *qāḍī* court, in order to

"obtain their dowries according to the *sheriat*"[51] and to make "agreements concerning the

maintenance allowance of their children."[52] Among the court records studied by Gradeva

are several cases between Christian parties, such as recorded contracts between relatives,

property disputes between parents and children, and announcements of marriages and

divorces.[53] Gradeva puts forward different reasons why Christians in some instances

preferred the *qāḍī* court over their own court:

"Some Christians sought to take advantage of the more favourable stipulations of the

---

[50] Ibid.

[51] Rossita Gradeva, "Orthodox Christians in the Kadi Courts: The Practice of the Sofia Sheriat Courts, Seventeenth Century," *Islamic Law and Society* 4 (1997): p. 68. See also Shaham, Ron. "Jews and the Shari'a Courts in Modern Egypt." *Studia Islamica* 82 (1995): 113–136.

[52] Ibid.

[53] Ibid.

sheriat or its lower fees, or obtains a document that might provide them with security

with respect to Ottoman officials or anyone who might contest their ownership rights or

marital status. Others were not satisfied with the church courts and preferred to seek

justice from the kadı, whose judicial powers were supported by the state, which had the

power to enforce his decision, ...".[54]

Furthermore, while the non-legal sphere of the Sharia is governed by the ethical *al-ahkām al-shar'iyya*[55] scale with its five categories, the legal Sharia is governed by a purely legal scale that differentiates only between the validity (*ṣaḥīḥ*) or the nullity (*bāṭil*) of a certain act.[56]

In terms of content, we can also identify a substantial overlap concerning the fields covered by the legal Sharia and Western law. Among others, these fields include marriage, inheritance, contracts, penal law, evidence and procedure, and the definition of obligations and rights of legal subjects. Additionally, customary practice plays a role in both legal systems as well and the Sharia recognized local custom to a sometimes larger or smaller degree, as long as it did not contradict the Sharia. If for example a marriage contract is silent on the due date of the payment of the dower (*mahr*), then, in case of a dispute the judge would rely on the local custom.[57]

The general rule of recognition – rules that inform the legal subject about what a valid legal rule is – in the Islamic legal system is that "a valid rule is one given by God,

---

[54] Ibid.

[55] God's instructions (*taklīf*, obligation or duty) to humanity come in the form of either commands or prohibition that entail reward in the hereafter in the case of abiding by his instructions and punishment in the hereafter, when one disobeys his instructions. In that regard, each act is subsumed under one of five categories (*al-aḥkām al-shar'iyya*). Accordingly, an act can be obligatory (*wājib*) or forbidden (*ḥarām*), in which case obedience is rewarded and disobedience is punished; or an act is recommended (*mandūb*) or reprehensible (*makrūh*), in which case compliance is rewarded, but non-compliance is not punished; or finally, an act is just neutral (*mubāḥ*), meaning that it neither entails reward, nor punishment. The default in the absence of a text is that acts are seen as belonging to the neutral category (*al-aṣl fī al-ashyā' al-ibāḥa*). See Peters and Bearman, "Introduction: The Nature of the Sharia," p. 1-2.

[56] Baber Johansen, *Contingency in a Sacred Law: Legal and Ethical Norms in the Muslim Fiqh* (Leiden: Brill, 1999), p. 70.

[57] Peters and Bearman, "Introduction: The Nature of the Sharia," p. 5.

---

through his revealed sources."[58] Since there is not a clear rule on every question to be found in the revealed sources and the state was not allowed to create the Sharia, jurists developed the legal discipline called *uṣūl al-fiqh*, meaning legal methodology, legal epistemology, or principles of jurisprudence. That discipline laid out the guidelines according to which injunctions should be derived from the revealed sources. In that light, we can specify the rule of recognition in the Islamic legal system, by saying that norms must be derived by jurists from the revealed sources in accordance with *uṣūl al-fiqh*.[59]

However, even this as a rule of thumb is not specific enough in the context of the Sharia. Due to the complete lack of a central authority in Sunni Islam, there was and still is a vast plurality of even sometimes contradicting opinions. The Sunni Islamic legal tradition recognizes four different schools of jurisprudence (*madhhab*) as equally valid and in the past there used to be more than just those four schools. Those schools played an important role in restricting the independent endeavor of jurists in deriving rules from the revealed sources (*ijtihād*). Scholars in each school had to take the existing opinions of their previous generations of scholars in to account and even had to follow them (*taqlīd*).[60] Fadel calls this "the crystallization of legal doctrine", referring to the process of homogenization of the schools' legal views, which he demonstrates through the example of the *mālikī* school.[61]

At the same time the differences between the schools remained. Therefore, in order to be as specific as possible with regards to what a rule of recognition in an Islamic legal system is, we have to point out that this can only be said for each respective school. Thus, "a valid and enforceable norm is the one that is recognized as authoritative by the jurists

---

[58] Ibid., p. 6.

[59] Ibid. It is important to note that such an understanding excludes notions of justice that are not explicitly derived from scripture, such as legal arrangements legislated under the doctrine of *siyāsa*. This will be subject to discussion in chapter Three.

[60] Ibid.

[61] Mohammad Fadel, "The Social Logic of *Taqlīd* and the Rise of the *Mukhtaṣar*," *Islamic Law and Society* 3 (1996): particularly p. 219 ff.

following that particular school."[62]

This kind of partial-uniformity is important when we take into account that judges as a rule were required to follow their affiliated legal school (*madhhab*) in their adjudication. In that regard the 'crystallization of the school doctrine' was crucial, as it contributed to a certain amount of legal certainty.[63]

The "restriction" of the school of jurisprudence to four[64] and the fact that with the "closure of the gate of *ijtihād*" no new school was to be founded and exist aside from the four, coupled with the "crystallization of each schools' doctrine" can be seen as further examples of restraining ambiguity up to a manageable amount. Here, the predictability of the law. Despite those steps to decrease ambiguity, there is still a fair amount of pluralism and tolerance for ambiguity, which is expressed in the doctrine "*kull mujtahid muṣīb*". According to this doctrine the legal outcome of every *mujtahids'* (a person who engages in *ijtihād*) pursue for a legal question is equally acceptable even if only one answer is correct in the sense that it corresponds to the law in the mind of God. In each case, every *mujtahid* who engaged in the endeavor of *ijtihād* would still receive divine reward and is allowed to follow his own legal result, but the reward of the *mujtahid* who reached the "correct" answer – correct in the sense that his answer overlaps with the one in God's mind – his reward will be higher.[65]

Notion of Change

If Muslims believe that God is the only legitimate lawgiver (*shāri*'), who has

---

[62] Peters and Bearman, "Introduction: The Nature of the Sharia," p. 6.

[63] Ibid. For further information, look at Ibrahim, Ahmed Fekry. *Pragmatism in Islamic law: A Social and Intellectual History*. Syracuse: Syracuse University Press, 2015.

[64] The four *madhhabs* up to this day are the *Ḥanafiyya*, the *Mālikiyya*, the *Shāfiiyya ī* and the *Ḥanbaliyya*. They are all characterized by having an eponym figure and their own distinct legal methodology.

[65] Bauer, *Die Kultur der Ambiguität*, p. 176-177; Ahmed Fekry Ibrahim, *Pragmatism in Islamic law: A Social and Intellectual History* (Syracuse: Syracuse University Press, 2015), p. 31 ff.

revealed a "perfect set of rules (Q 6:154)" in his last scripture to the Prophet, with whose death communication between God and humankind came to an end, then the idea of changing God's perfect law would be inconceivable for the believer. Even though the Sharia is flexible and underwent change, this in fact poses a challenge to Muslim jurists, especially with regards to clear and detailed rules found in the scriptural sources, where interpretation is the only way of "alteration".[66]

In order to create a legal system that could do both address issues of their time and tackle questions yet to come, scholars used different hermeneutics that enabled them to extent what they found in the finite body of scripture.[67] Rohe observes that from the early days it was humans who constructed the law by interpretation of texts, extending of known rules and the way they implemented them. He makes a valid point when he writes that the claim made by many scholars, "that God alone could be the 'lawgiver', ultimately has no validity."[68]

Some of those hermeneutic techniques used in that human endeavor and that continue to play a very fundamental role in Islamic law are *qiyās* (analogy), *istiḥsān* (equitable discretion), *sadd al-dharā'i'* (blocking the means), *maṣlaḥa mursala* (general welfare independent of scripture), *qawā'id fiqhiyya*, and *tarjīḥ*. These kinds of techniques assume the rationality of the law, otherwise the use of analogy for example could not be justified.[69]

We can also observe that aside from just extending existing "laws" found in

---

[66] Peters and Bearman, "Introduction: The Nature of the Sharia," p. 7.

[67] Umar F. Abd-Allah, "Theological Dimensions of Islamic Law," in *The Cambridge Companion to Classical Islamic Theology*, ed. Tim Winter. (Cambridge: Cambridge University Press, 2008), p. 239.

[68] Rohe, Islamic Law in Past and Present, p. 19.

[69] Abd-Allah, "Theological Dimensions of Islamic Law," p. 246. For a presentation of different Muslim accounts on this issue look at Reinhart, A. Kevin. "Ritual Action and Practical Action: The Incomprehensibility of Muslim Devotional Action." In *Islamic Law in Theory: Studies on Jurisprudence in Honor of Bernard Weiss*, edited by A. Kevin Reinhart and Robert Gleave, 55-103. Leiden: Brill, 2014.

scripture, jurists wrote extensively about the purpose of the law. Every new norm that was

for example the result of an analogy, would be dismissed if it would go against the

purposes and aims of the law. However, in terms of rationality of the law jurists

distinguished between matters that were accessible to reason, such as non-ritualistic

matters (*mu'āmalāt*), and matters that were not accessible to reason, such as rituals proper

(ibadat).[70] The formalities of rituals are independent of time or place, and are thereby not

open to modification. It is also impossible to understand the rationale behind the

prohibition of pork, the movements during the ritual prayer and the specifics of ablution.[71]

Non-ritualistic matters on the other hand are supposed to have legal rationales according to

jurists, and were subject to modification for the sake of retaining their purpose as is

expressed in the following legal maxim (*qā'ida* sg. of *qawā'id*):" Modifications of legal

judgments will not be denounced when they reflect changing times, places and

circumstances."[72]

The purpose of the law was to guarantee the well-being of humans and because of

that *ijtihād* was necessary in order to make sure that the law would fulfill its purpose in an

ever changing world.[73] The different Sunni schools of jurisprudence all accepted most of

the above mentioned rational instruments to a bigger or lesser degree in their law-

making.[74] They would differ in the limit and scope of the applicability of several

hermeneutics and the hierarchy and relationship between each source and hermeneutic.

Legal practice shows that the Islamic legal system was flexible enough in reacting

---

[70] Rohe, Islamic Law in Past and Present, p. 19.

[71] Abd-Allah, "Theological Dimensions of Islamic Law," p. 241-242. Matters that are fixed by revelation like the prohibition of eating pork. One can speculate about the reason behind the prohibition, but since the scholar cannot know what the true motivation behind God's dicta was, he cannot modify the ruling.

[72] Ibid., p. 244.

[73] Ibid.

[74] Ibid., p. 246.

to and accommodating social change.[75] According to Vishanoff, this was possible because the "law-oriented hermeneutical paradigm" of al-Shāfiʿī maximized interpretive flexibility in a way that scholars were "able to imagine their system of legal rules as revealed and thus divinely authoritative, even as they continued to adapt those laws to changing social contexts."[76] However, if we would not conceive of the Sharia as a body of rules, but rather as something more abstract, such as a system of principles, or a system of protected interests, then it would not be a surprise that rules have to change in order to remain true to their purpose.

What we said so far assumes *fiqh* as the only legitimate manifestation of the Sharia and sees the monopoly of law-making in the hands of *madrasa* educated jurists. Discussions involving *siyāsa, qanūn,* the silence of the law and notions of justice outside of explicit texts of scripture are missing so far in our discussion. Therefore, what will be of particular interest in this paper is to look at all the actors involved in the law-making process. Who initiates the process? With all of this (relative) pluralism in mind, who has the final say? Further questions that will show up in the course of seeking answers to these questions are, whether or not Islamic law is fixed, because it is derived from fixed and limited revealed texts? Or would it be more appropriate to regard Islamic law as a set of principles, values and a system comprising legally protected interests? Even further and of crucial importance are questions regarding notions of equity; are only explicit texts found in scripture a legitimate source or are there other sources and notions of justice allowed as well? In that regard we have to include a discussion of *siyāsa, qanūn,* discretion, the spirit of the law and their place and relationship with Sharia.

---

[75] Peters and Bearman, "Introduction: The Nature of the Sharia," p. 7.
[76] David R. Vishanoff, The Formation of Islamic Hermeneutics: How Sunni Legal Theorists Imagined a Revealed Law, (New Haven: American Oriental Society, 2011), p. 3.

Talal Asad's characterization of Islam as a "discursive tradition" seems meaningful for our discussion:

"A tradition consists essentially of discourses that seek to instruct practitioners regarding the correct form and purpose of a given practice that, precisely because it is established, has a history. These discourses relate conceptually to a past (when the practice was instituted, and from which the knowledge of its point and proper performance has been transmitted) and a future (how the point of that practice can best be secured in the short or long term, or why it should be modified or abandoned), through a present (how it is linked to other practices, institutions, and social conditions)."[77]

"… there cannot be a universal definition of religion, not only because its constituent elements and relationships are historically specific, but because that definition is itself the historical product of discursive processes."[78]

Asad lists several actors who participate in this discourse, such as the *'ulamā'*, preachers, Sufi *shuyūkh*, or unlettered parents.[79] Moreover, part of an anthropology of Islam is the interaction of those different actors at different times, places and contexts (political, socio-economic, etc.), with each other and their environment, whether it is in order to "regulate, uphold, require, or adjust correct practices, and to condemn, exclude, undermine, or replace incorrect ones,"[80] which also includes "the resistances they encounter (from Muslims and non-Muslims)."[81] As a consequence, the high level of

---

[77] Talal Asad, "The Idea of an Anthropology of Islam," *Qui Parle* 17 (2009): p. 20.
[78] Talal Asad, *Genealogies of Religion: Discipline and Reasons of Power in Christianity and Islam* (Baltimore: The Johns Hopkins University Press, 1993), p. 29.
[79] Asad, "The Idea of an Anthropology of Islam," p. 21.
[80] Ibid., p. 22.
[81] Ibid.

ambiguity and heterogeneity we face in Islamic traditions is only natural, along with the concomitant arguments and disputes over the "form and significance of practices."[82]

In regards to Islamic law, its sources, its "correct" form, content and application, we should not restrict ourselves to juristic discourse only, but conceive of further actors, such as the ruler, his agents and the laity among others, as equally legitimate participants in the overall discourse of Islamic law. Furthermore, such as Shahab Ahmed proposed that Islam should be conceptualized "as and in terms of *process*"[83], the same should be equally valid for Islamic law.

Conclusion

A lot of the above-mentioned points make sense in a framework of Islamic law that is limited to the scriptural sources and laws derived through them by jurists in accordance with *uṣūl al-fiqh*. But we have to acknowledge that the Koran and the *ḥadīth*-literature do not cover every imaginable area and it is hard, not to say impossible, to always find a "precedent" that could serve for a meaningful *qiyās*. So, what is about the silence of the Sharia, the silence of revealed sources? If *qiyās* is not the only possible and legitimate way to develop the law, then we have to look at concepts like juristic discretion (*istiḥsān*), public good (*maṣlaḥa*), maxims (*qawā ʿid*) and the role of the spirit of the law. In the following chapters, we will come across several of those concepts and how jurists used them in the history of Islamic law.

Furthermore, in this chapter we showed that generalizations of Islamic law as being an irrational, rigid, and all-encompassing law are either not or only partly applicable to

---

[82] Ibid. See also page 23 in idem. "The variety of traditional Muslim practices in different times, places, and populations indicate the different Islamic reasonings that different social and historical conditions can or cannot sustain."

[83] Shahab Ahmed, *What is Islam?: The Importance of Being Islamic* (Princeton: Princeton University Press, 2016), p. 117. For more on this discussion and his critiques of Asad's and others' conception of Islam, and his own proposal of what Islam is, see idem.

Islamic law. We should regard Islamic law as a legal system and view it in the way we study any other kind of law or legal system. In this thesis, we will be concerned with Islamic law in the strictly legal sense.

CHAPTER TWO

In his typology of Islamic law Max Weber comes to the conclusion that Islamic law is deficient and he characterizes it as not only unable, but also unwilling to accommodate changing social circumstances, especially after the closure of the gate of independent reasoning *(ijtihād)*. According to him this reached a state, where Islamic law became inapplicable to a continuously growing number of areas of the social life and thereby failed to offer legal predictability and was incapable of regulating the society. These shortcomings rendered Islamic law irrelevant to reality. In Weber's view, Islamic law was therefore a merely unachievable ideal and not practical for governance. His notion of Islamic law predated what "Orientalists" would have to say about Islamic law. Some of the common themes and motives are the difference between religious- and secular law, the tension between legal ideas and reality, legal change versus stagnation, and formally rational law against substantively rational law.[84]

The term "Orientalists" is used here in the way that Edward Said coined the term. He offers three interdependent meanings in his definition of "Orientalism". He identifies that the scholarship of European Orientalists is characterized by an unquestioned dichotomy between an imagined Orient and the Occident, in which the people and civilizations of the East and the West are understood as being different and even opposing

---

[84] Mohammad Fadel, "State and the Sharia," in *The Ashgate Research Companion to Islamic Law*, ed. Rudolph Peters et al. (Surrey: Ashgate Publishing Press, 2014), p. 94.

entities. The Orient is constructed as the "other".[85] This kind of thinking is inherent in the way Europeans dealt with the Orient:

> "dealing with it by making statements about it, authorizing views of it, describing it, by teaching it, settling it, ruling over it: in short, Orientalism as a Western style for dominating, restructuring and having authority over the Orient."[86]

When we speak about the field of Islamic law the most famous "Orientalists" would be Ignaz Goldziher (d. 1921 CE), Joseph Schacht (d. 1969 CE) and Noel Coulson (1986 CE), who view Islamic law as the opposing other of Western legal systems. Whereas Western law is described in terms such as evolving or secular, Islamic law is seen as the opposite, that is immutable, fixed and religious. [87]

In what follows we will have a closer look at two of those mentioned scholars, Joseph Schacht and Noel Coulson. Shalakany finds those two scholars as the best representatives of what he calls the dominant, standard Western approach to the history of Islamic law, dominant historiography. Albeit, he is aware that there are major differences between their scholarship, Shalakany points out that their scholarship shares some very fundamental premises. In his argument, he focuses on two seminal works, namely Schacht's *An Introduction to Islamic law* and Coulson's *A History of Islamic Law*. Shalakany distills four premises from those works, which in his opinion represent the mainstay of the dominant historiography's framework that he argues is still largely intact. Furthermore, he argues that those two mentioned books still enjoy a high status as foundational material in reading lists in the field.[88] Shalakany echoes what Knut Vikor

---

[85] Edward W. Said, *Orientalism* (New York: Vintage Books, 1979), p. 2-3.
[86] Ibid., p. 3.
[87] Shalakany, "Islamic Legal Histories," p. 29.
[88] Ibid., p. 5.

wrote in the preface of his monograph *Between God and the Sultan*, which was published

in the year 2005, just three years before the release of Shalakany's article. In his preface, it

reads as follows:

> "This is probably the first introductory textbook to the history of Islamic law to appear
> in English since 1964. Given the rapid expansion of research in this field over the last
> decades, this fact is a lasting testimony to the two great works that appeared in that
> year, Neil Coulson's History of Islamic law and in particular Joseph Schacht's
> magisterial Introduction to Islamic law. The lasting quality of these works has made it
> difficult to consider the need or indeed possibility for any replacement to them."[89]

Even though, Shalakany agrees that Said's definition of "Orientalism" applies to

Schacht and Coulson as well[90], he sees "Scripturalism"[91] as another very important

paradigm that underlies their scholarship and that is better suited to describe the premises

of what he calls "the dominant historiography" of Islamic law. The dominant

historiography is characterized by a dichotomy between religious law *(sharīʿah)* based on

scripture and man-made secular law (*siyāsa*), and the dichotomy between tradition and

modernity. Thereby, the only things that fall into the category of "Islamic law in history" is

the Koran, the Sunna and jurists' treatises expounding on these two scriptural sources. This

implies further that "a lot of what your average American … lawyer would take for legal

history happens to fall outside the dominant plot of Islamic law historiography."[92]

In the following two chapters, we will deal with the first two of the four premises of

---

[89] Knut Vikør, *Between God and the Sultan: A History of Islamic Law* (London: Hurst & Company, 2005), p. vi.

[90] Shalakany, "Islamic Legal Histories," p. 28-33.

[91] Regarding the term "Scripturalism" that Shalakany borrowed from Clifford Geertz, see Shalakany, "Islamic Legal Histories," p. 33-39.

[92] Ibid., p. 5-6. See further on page 6: "This would include among others commercial customs, administrative rules of the Abbasid bureaucracy, criminal justice measures of the Mamluk rulers, or the norms and structures of Ottoman political governance."

the dominant historiography in more detail. The first two premises according to Shalakany are the following: Islamic law is Shariʿa and Shariʿa is not Siyasa.[93] What concerns us here is first of all what is understood as Sharia in this context and the implications those premises carry in terms of who are the actors involved in the law-making process, what are legitimate sources for the law-making process and what counts as sources for the study of the history of Islamic law.

In order to fully comprehend the framework of the dominant historiography, we will have to talk about what is understood by the dominant historiography as a quasi-constitutional arrangement between the religious scholars (ʿālim, pl. ʿulamā ʾ) and the state, after the former emerged victorious against the latter. According to that vision of separation of powers only the ʿulamā ʾ possessed the license to "produce" the law and the state's role in that process was reduced to the enforcement and execution of that body of laws. For now, that short explanation suffices and we shall revisit this issue in chapter Three.

Premise One of the Dominant Historiography

Shalakany draws attention to the structure of both Schacht's and Coulson's books on Islamic law and their terminology used throughout them. They use the terms Islamic Law and Sharia interchangeably. For example, Schacht mainly uses the term Islamic law to

---

[93] Ibid., p. 5. The third premise is that the Sharia/*siyāsa* dichotomy based on premises one and two defines the nature of Islamic law as a historical phenomenon up to the colonial encounter. (See idem. p. 16-21.) Premise four then revolves around the dichotomy between tradition and modernity that is used to explain the development of Islamic law from the colonial encounter onwards up till now. (See idem. p. 28-33.);

Rohe, *Islamic Law in Past and Present*, p. 42: Generally, the ruler was allowed and even obliged by the Sharia to make administrative and political decisions for the public good. As such, the *siyāsa* of the ruler is part of the Sharia if it serves towards that end;

Yossef Rapoport, "Royal Justice and Religious Law: *Siyāsah* and Shariʿah under the Mamluks," *Mamluk Studies Review* 16 (2012): p. 77: Yet, in the writings of jurists we often see a terminological difference between the *sharʿ* as the divine law and *siyāsa* as the administration of justice.

For examples, what some jurists had to say on the relationship between Sharia and *siyāsa*, and particularly on the doctrine of *siyāsa al-sharʿiyya* see chapter Three below.

describe his subject of inquiry and only occasionally does he use the Arabic term, Sharia, which he employs as a synonym for Islamic law. Coulson uses both terms interchangeably as well, however, he almost exclusively utilizes the term Sharia instead of Islamic law. Furthermore, except for Schacht's glossary, a definition of either term is absent. Neither Sharia, nor Islamic law is defined in their introduction or in any of their books' chapters.[94] As for Schacht's glossary-definition of the word Sharia, he writes the following:

"shar', shari'a, the sacred Law of Islam,...opposed to siyāsa, administrative justice.."[95]

According to this understanding the sacred law of Islam is called *"shar'"* or *"shari'a"* and it is not *siyāsa* or administrative justice.[96] Schacht argues that Islamic law is "an all-embracing body of religious duties, the totality of Allah's commands that regulate the life of every Muslim in all its aspects; it comprises on an equal footing ordinances regarding worship and ritual, as well as political and (in the narrow sense) legal rules."[97] In Islamic law God is regarded as the sole legislator, and in order to stay true to this claim of divine authority, jurists tried to confine the "human element" in form of personal opinion to strict analogy on the basis of the divine material sources. Even this mode of reasoning came to end once the doctrine of the "closure of the gate of *ijtihād*" was established. Schacht viewed this "traditionalism" of the law as the "most essential feature...typical of a 'sacred law'."[98] Because of that, the law "called for the observance of the letter rather than of the spirit" of the law.[99] A further characteristic of the sacred law of Islam was that it contains a few "heteronomous and irrational features."[100] Moreover, as a

---

[94] Ibid., p. 10.
[95] Schacht, *An Introduction to Islamic Law*, p. 302.
[96] Shalakany, "Islamic Legal Histories," p. 10.
[97] Schacht, *An Introduction to Islamic Law*, p. 1.
[98] Ibid., p. 211.
[99] Ibid., p. 204.
[100] Ibid., p. 202.

sacred law based on divine sources, the law was disconnected from the needs of society: "The formation of Islamic law took neither place under the impetus of the needs of practice, nor under that of judicial technique, but under that of religious and ethical ideas."[101] And "considerations of good faith, fairness, justice, truth..."[102] occupied a very subordinate role in the law, compared to "religious and ethical considerations."[103] As such, even law proper was integrated into a system of religious duties, which assesses "all human acts and relationships, including those which we call legal, from the point of view of the concepts obligatory/recommended/indifferent/reprehensible/forbidden."[104]

Coulson agrees with several of those points when talking about Islamic law as a sacred law, such as on the point that Islamic law is disconnected from the needs and the practice of the society: "Law, in classical Islamic theory, is the revealed will of God, a divinely ordained system preceding and not preceded by the Muslim state, controlling and not controlled by Muslim society. There can thus be no notion of the law itself evolving as an historical phenomenon closely tied with the progress of society."[105] A further characteristic of Islamic law, as a divine law, according to Coulson is that "it is a rigid and immutable system, embodying norms of an absolute and eternal validity, which are not susceptible to modification by any legislative authority."[106]

It is very striking to notice that both scholars use the terms "*shari'a*" and "Islamic law" synonymously. Furthermore, they constantly refer to Sharia as being a "religious", "divine" or "sacred" law, derived from scriptures, that express God's will and that was revealed to the Prophet Muhammad. Since Schacht and Coulson do not make a distinction

---

[101] Ibid., p. 209.
[102] Ibid., p. 203.
[103] Ibid., p. 201.
[104] Ibid., p. 200.
[105] Coulson, *A History of Islamic Law*, p. 1-2.
[106] Ibid., p. 5.

between Sharia and Islamic law it is just logical to say that the same characterization of

Sharia holds true for Islamic law as well.[107] As we will see this assumption has very

substantial implications for the study of Islamic Law.

If we assume that the history of Islamic law is the history of Sharia, then this

answers the question regarding "…what makes past law deserve historical study as Islamic

law."[108] As mentioned above Sharia is derived from a set of revealed scriptural sources and

there exists a "particular theory of jurisprudence" that offers a definition of those

normative scriptural sources and an explanation of the allowed techniques to derive rulings

out of them. When Schacht and Coulson talk about that theory they refer to the concept of

uṣūl al-fiqh.[109] This demonstrates that they, just like most premodern jurists, do not draw a

distinction between Sharia and *fiqh*.[110]

Since God is the only legitimate legislator, whose law is embedded in scripture,

jurists use *uṣūl al-fiqh* in order to discover that law. Islamic law or the Sharia therefore has

its direct basis in scripture (only), the Koran and the prophetic tradition, or in consensus

(*ijmā*ʿ), or is derived from these sources through analogical reasoning (*qiyās*).[111]

---

[107] Shalakany, "Islamic Legal Histories," p. 10.

[108] Ibid., p. 11.

[109] Ibid.

[110] Ibrahim, *Pragmatism in Islamic law*, p. 2: "The word *Sharīʿa* is most often used in the primary sources to mean simply substantive law, but sometimes (especially in the modern period) a clear distinction is drawn between Sharīʿa, which is divine law as lodged in the mind of God, and fiqh, human approximations and understanding of the divine ideal." Although, jurists might claim that their rules of *fiqh* are the only legitimate expression of the Sharia as divine law, one has to be cautious not to take their viewpoints on those matters at face value: "A vital issue (both Islamically and otherwise) is to ask how the scholars' representations, their doctrines, are a function of their efforts to consolidate fiqh's control over power, or—what is from their perspective the same thing—to advance their own authority over other social forces. For all these reasons sound method demands that we approach an Islamic legal system from more than one angle, separately according to the differing perspectives of its various actors ", in Frank E. Vogel, *Islamic Law and Legal System: Studies of Saudi Arabia* (Leiden: Brill, 2000), p. 171. For further information on the competition between jurists and rulers, or *fiqh* and *siyāsa*, see below, chapter Three, and Vogel, Frank E. "The Rule of Law in Saudi Arabia: Exploring Contradictions and Traditions." In *The Rule of Law in the Middle East and the Islamic World: Human Rights and the Judicial Process*, edited by Cotran Eugene and Yamani Mai, 128-136. London: I.B. Tauris, 2000.
Regarding Schacht and Coulson, we can say that due to the availability of sources they relied heavily on jurists authored works and the tropes of jurists. For example, one "fiction" in the writings of jurists consulted by Schacht, which is fundamental for his narrative on Islamic law, and that we will deal with in more detail below, is the "closure of the gate of ijtihad". Intisar Rabb, *Doubt in Islamic Law: A History of Legal Maxims, Interpretation, and Islamic Criminal Law* (New York: Cambridge University Press, 2015), p. 9, and note 16 on page 9; Behnam Sadeghi, *The Logic of Law Making in Islam: Women and Prayer in the Legal Tradition* (Cambridge: Cambridge University Press, 2013), p. 164-165.

[111] Shalakany, "Islamic Legal Histories," p 11.

The jurist has to consult these four sources whenever he seeks an answer for a legal problem. This process is called *ijtihād* and is explained by Schacht and Coulson in the following manner. The Koran is the first source the jurist consults in order to find a divine law for a question at hand. Should he not find one there, he is supposed to look into the second divine source, the Sunna, more specifically the six canonical *hadīth* collections (*al-kutub al-sitta*). If this does not provide an answer as well, he should turn to the third source, consensus.[112]

Usually those three sources will not have a ready rule for most legal issues, especially regarding issues that arose with more temporal distance towards the scriptural sources. That is why the fourth source (*qiyās*) the jurist has to resort to, is maybe the most important source in the process of deriving law.[113] Such a conception of Sharia places very substantial limits to the scope of the law, since even in the case of the fourth source, there is not always a basis in scripture to draw a meaningful analogy to every imaginable legal question, such as the question regarding the compilation and redaction of the Koran in a written form.

Periodization of Islamic Law

Schacht divides the history of Islamic law into "three principal stages" (periods). The first of those he calls the "formative" period, which he dates from the death of the prophet (632 CE) to the middle of the ninth century. This period was characterized by the conflict between parties who bore different conceptions of Islamic law, namely the people of opinion (*ahl al-ra'y*) and the people of tradition (*ahl al-hadīth*). By the end, 850 CE, of the

---

[112] Ibid., p. 11. The six collections are those of al-Bukhārī (d. 869 CE), Muslim (d. 874 CE), Abū Dāwud (d. 889 CE), al-Tirmidhī (d. 892 CE), al-Nasā'ī (d. 915 CE), and Ibn Māja (d. 887 CE).

[113] Ibid., p. 12. Analogy here means that the *ratio legis* (*'illa*) of a case/ruling that is found in scripture is extended towards a similar case. For instance, the Koran prohibits the consumption of wine. Jurists identified the intoxicating effect of wine as the *ratio legis* for its prohibition, and therefore they extended the Koranic prohibition of wine to every intoxicating substance including those, which are not explicitly mentioned in scripture, such as beer, vodka, etc.

formative period this conflict came to an end.[114] As a result, *fiqh* reached its peak (and

highest degree), and each of the four schools of jurisprudence (*madhhab*) acquired a legal

theory. Furthermore, it was around the end of that period (around the mid ninth century

CE) that every judge had to adjudicate according to the dominant views of his respective

school of jurisprudence.[115]

Uṣūl al-fiqh of al-Shāfiʿī

The jurist al-Shāfiʿī is attributed a fundamental role in the transition from the formative

period to the classical period by both Schacht and Coulson.[116] Especially when we talk

about legal methodology of Islamic law *(uṣūl al-fiqh)* it is incumbent to look at al-Shāfiʿī

(d. 820 CE), who is viewed by Schacht as the "master architect of Islamic law". According

to him the four primary sources of the law are the following: The Koran, the Sunna,

analogical reasoning *(qiyās)* and consensus *(ijmāʿ)*. The Koran and the Sunna represent the

revelation and its relevant content for the law can be seen as the raw material in the process

of the derivation of laws *(ijtihād)*. Through human endeavor that is applied on the legal

texts of the revelation the rules of the law are developed. In this process of systematization

analogical reasoning is one of the most fundamental tools in the repertoire of the jurist. The

product of this endeavor does not have the rank of law, but is instead a potential legal rule

among several other possible potential rulings, which could even be contradictory,

although they are based on the same text of revelation. We can speak of competing rules

that are found in the different schools of jurisprudence (*madhhab* sg. of *madhāhib*). Inside

each *madhhab,* the scholars select the view that is considered to be the best rule to follow.

This is decided by way of consensus within the legal schools, where applicable law is

---

[114] Ibid., p. 12.
[115] Ibid.
[116] Ibid.

determined out of a subset of competing potential rules.[117]

With his thesis, al-Shāfiʿī intended to create a middle position between two prevalent trends at his time and aimed to reconcile them. Those two parties were the two aforementioned groups, the people of *ḥadīth (ahl al-ḥadīth)* and the people of opinion *(ahl al-raʾy)*. The former can be seen as a reaction to the latter. The people of *ḥadīth* criticized the people of opinion, because according to their view the law of the people of opinion was not mainly based on revelation. In contrast to them, they wanted the law to rest upon revealed texts only. However, concerning new cases that were not established in the scripture, the people of *ḥadīth* could not offer as much practicality as the people of opinion. Al-Shāfiʿī aimed to offer a systematized law that is both Islamic and practical by using analogical reasoning in order to link practice to revelation, which allowed him to extent the legislation of the revelation to new cases that are not mentioned in the revealed texts.[118] Al-Shāfiʿī's thesis affected all other schools of law up to the point that scholars generally assume that:

> "all the four mazhabs of fiqh came into a consensus on the above four sources of shari'a, although some disagreement remained in ordering the importance of secondary sources of law among jurists of the four mazhabs."[119]

A very important change in comparison to his contemporary and past counterparts of the *mālikī* and *ḥanafī* tradition, was al-Shāfiʿī's different approach to Sunna and *ḥadīth*. While according to the former's understanding, *ḥadīth* and the Sunna of the prophet and his companions was embedded and conserved in the local practice of those communities[120]

---

[117] Vikør, *Between God and the Sultan*, p. 31-32.

[118] Ibid., p. 64-65.

[119] Shalakany, "Islamic Legal Histories," p. 13.

[120] In the case of the *mālikīs*, community refers to the people of Medina. For the *ḥanafīs* community does not include the masses, but primarily the scholars, who carry the religious tradition. See p. 51. in El Shamsy, Ahmed. *The Canonization of Islamic Law: A Social and Intellectual History*. Cambridge: Cambridge University

where the prophet, and after his death, his companions used to live. Al-Shafi'ī on the other hand, required a text with a sound chain of transmission for a such a practice to be normative – for him even a solitary report (*khabar wāhid*) was sufficient.[121] In addition, he criticized the *hanafiyya* and the *mālikiyya* for their legal methodology and use of non-scriptural sources. According to his understanding the scholars of the *hanafiyya* relied more on human reasoning instead on scripture by their use of *istihsān* and he dismissed the *mālikī* concept of ʿamal as not trustworthy. By following the practice of the people of Madina one cannot truly know which practices are of prophetic origin and this concept failed to offer coherent results.[122] Al-Shāfiʿī's theory viewed scriptural sources as the only valid basis for the law and he did not allow human reason outside the concept of *qiyās*.

Taqlīd

The third part of Schacht's (and Coulson's) periodization of pre-modern Islamic legal history is called the ("post-classical") "*taqlīd* period", which is supposed to have begun around the tenth century CE and lasted until 1798 CE, the date of Napoleon's invasion of Egypt. In Schacht's and Coulson's view this era marks the end point where independent reasoning (*ijtihād*) came to an end and this period is thereby characterized according to their understanding with the occurring of a shift from *ijtihād* to *taqlīd*. Meaning that jurists were bound by the opinions of their respective schools of jurisprudence. In that regard this period is associated with the famous expression "closure of the gate of *ijtihād*". From that point on no formation of a new school would be allowed[123] and from the tenth century

---

Press, 2013.

[121] Ahmed El Shamsy, *The Canonization of Islamic Law: A Social and Intellectual History* (Cambridge: Cambridge University Press, 2013), p. 49-50.

[122] Ibid., p. 64-65. Shamsy describes Mālik's concept of ʿamal as a "black box", meaning that this concept fails to distinguish whether a certain practice of the people of Madina originated with the prophet or not. It only tells us that a certain practice is practiced by the people of Madina.

[123] Shalakany, "Islamic Legal Histories," p. 13.

onwards "every jurist was an 'imitator' (*muqalllid*) bound to accept and follow the doctrine established by his predecessors."[124] What does the "closure of the gate of *ijtihād*" mean for Schacht and Coulson?

It means that during that period of *"taqlīd"* legal change was (almost) impossible and the law ossified. Scholars of the study of Islamic law who came to that conclusion relied primarily on the study of "canonical" legal compendia of the four schools of law that were composed by jurists. In addition to those works they looked at commentaries on those compendia and collections of legal opinions (*fatāwā*). All those genres are authored by the *'ulamā'* class, comprised of jurists and legal scholars. Thus, this study of Islamic Law can be described as the study of rules that are derived by religious scholars from the divine scriptural sources available in juristic texts.[125]

Conclusion of the First Premise

The first premise therefore equates Islamic law with the enterprise of jurists in the form of *fiqh*. The terms *fiqh* and Sharia are used as synonyms, which also means that Sharia, or *fiqh*, and by extension Islamic law is done by jurists and is thereby present in their writings. Consequently, Islamic law is what is derived by jurists from the divine sources Koran and *ḥadīth* through the four sources of *uṣūl al-fiqh,* whereby particularly al-Shāfiʿī's articulation of *uṣūl al-fiqh* is seen as an ideal type of Islamic legal theory. After a point in time this creative process stopped and there were no *mujtahids* anymore who were capable of applying the legal methodology of *uṣūl al-fiqh* directly on the divine sources. Instead, jurists now were bound to follow the doctrine of the previous generation of jurists.

Later scholars criticized a lot of what the dominant historiography had to say about

---

[124] Coulson, *A History of Islamic Law*, p. 80-81.
[125] Shalakany, "Islamic Legal Histories," p. 13-14.

Islamic law. Now we will look at how subsequent scholars received Schacht's and Coulson's narratives and whether their views stood undisputed or not.

Anti-Orientalist Variations and Refinements

The "old" scholarship was harshly criticized for some of their views of near eastern societies and accused of having pre-conceived notions about the "Orient". This stream of scholarship is often times characterized as "revisionist"[126] scholarship in distinction to "Orientalist" scholarship. A maybe more important reason for revising older scholarship was naturally the appearance of new sources to study and the access to courts records. In the following we want to look at the most important challenges of revisionist scholars against orientalist scholarship in the field of Islamic law. It should be noted that this will be a very selective picture of the mass of responses.

One of the first criticisms was regarding the periodization of the development of Islamic law. The dominant historiography assumes a linear narrative of progression and decline in three stages, the "formative period" with the resulting "classical theory", and the "*taqlīd*" period.[127] As part of that narrative the role of the "master architect" of Islamic law is attributed to al-Shāfiʿī. Regarding that, Bauer notes that a lot of central topics concerning *uṣūl al-fiqh* are absent from al-Shāfiʿī's (d. 820 CE) Risāla and therefore, it cannot be regarded as the last word on legal methodology. Instead, one should refer to Fakhraddīn Rāzī's (d. 1209 CE) *al-Maḥṣūl fī ʿilm al-Uṣūl* in order to get a "final" and comprehensive form of *uṣūl al-fiqh*. In this book the author synthesizes several works on *uṣūl al-fiqh* written by scholars before him. Rāzī's *Maḥṣūl* had a lasting impact in one way or another

---

[126] Not to be confused with other "revisionists". In fact, Orientalist scholarship is also revisionist in the sense that they completely or partly reject Muslim sources and narratives.

[127] Shalakany, "Islamic Legal Histories," p. 63.

on every book on legal methodology released after it.[128]

In addition to the mentioned primary sources there are also secondary sources of Islamic law, namely the concept of juristic preference *(istiḥsān)*, the idea of the common good *(maṣlaḥa)* and custom *('urf)*. *Istiḥsān* is especially relevant if a result of *qiyās* is deemed unreasonable or would have unexpected negative ramifications, such as the cutting off of the thief's hand. This rule is found in the text, but it does not provide any kinds of exemptions, as for example in extreme cases, where someone steals food, because he is dying from hunger.[129] The principle of *maṣlaḥa* used to have the same meaning as *istiḥsān*, but it changed over time and is described as *maṣlaḥa* that is independent from the text *(maṣlaḥa mursala)*. Rules derived using this principle are justified by social changes over time and necessities *(ḍarūra)* like for instance the collection and edition of the Koran. Even though there is no indication in the revelation that commands the collection of the Koran and moreover, there is no possible *qiyās* to justify it, jurists argued that it was a necessary task, in order to preserve and disseminate the revealed text.[130] The broader concept of *maṣlaḥa* is also often understood as public interest.[131] It should be noted that those secondary sources are not equally accepted throughout each of the four schools of jurisprudence. Nevertheless, they are very important tools for law making and they are also one factor in accounting for the different views among and between the four schools.

Another very important discussion revolves around the closure of the gate of *ijtihād*. Dominant historiography views this phenomenon as the stagnation of the law and assumes that after that point in time change in the law became (almost) impossible.[132] The

---

[128] Bauer, *Die Kultur der Ambiguität*, p. 22.

[129] Vikør, *Between God and the Sultan*, p. 66.

[130] Ibid., p. 68-69.

[131] For further reading on the role of Maṣlaḥa see Opwis, Felicitas. *Maṣlaḥa and the Purpose of the Law: Islamic Discourse on Legal Change from the 4th/10th to 8th/14th Century.* Leiden: Brill, 2010.

[132] Shalakany, "Islamic Legal Histories," p. 64.

question regarding the significance of the secondary sources of legal theory, such as custom or *maṣlaḥa mursala*, is related to the discussion of possible change in Islamic law during the period after the supposed "closure of the gate of *ijtihād*".[133] We will see the impact of those secondary sources in Islamic law in chapter Three.

Schacht and Coulson understood the *ijtihād/taqlīd* binary in the sense of legal change (*ijtihād*) on one side and rigidity (*taqlīd*) on the other side. Here, *taqlīd* carries a negative connotation and is seen as impeding legal change. Sherman Jackson showed through the concept of "legal scaffolding" that change during the "*taqlīd* period" was still possible and he associated *taqlīd* with legal predictability.[134]

Generally, Jackson argues that after the formative period, which was characterized by the hegemony of *ijtihād*, the two concepts *ijtihād* and *taqlīd* should be viewed as competing hegemonies in the history of Islamic law, without seeing them as mutually exclusive. Even though, *taqlīd* became more dominant at some point in time – Jackson pin points that shift to the 12th century – this did not make *ijtihād* or legal change impossible.[135]

The modes to achieve legal change became different, one could even say, it became more sophisticated, which runs counter to the claim that *taqlīd* led to decline in legal thought. In contrast to the formative period, which is characterized by less or no rules on specific issues, one can expect that it is easier to produce new rulings, under the reign of *taqlīd* however, the jurist had to take into account existing rules. Thus, in order to achieve

---

[133] Ibid., p. 66.

[134] Ahmed Fekry Ibrahim, "Rethinking the *Taqlīd* Hegemony: An Institutional, *Longue-Durée* Approach," Forthcoming: p. 1-2. For the first challenges against the notion of the "closure of the gate of *ijtihād*" see: Peters, Rudolph. "*Ijtihād* and *Taqlīd* in 18th and 19th Century." *Die Welt des Islam* 29 (1980): 131–145; Makdisi, George. *The Rise of Colleges: Institutions of Learning in Islam and the West.* Edinburgh: Edinburgh University Press, 1981; Hallaq, Wael B. "Was the Gate of *Ijtihād* Closed." *International Journal of Middle East Studies* 16 (1984): 3–41.

[135] Sherman Jackson, *Islamic Law and the State: The Constitutional Jurisprudence of Shihāb al-Dīn al-Qarāfī* (Leiden: Brill, 1996), p. 77.

legal change one could not just abandon an existing rule, but rather reinterpret it by classifying certain aspects of an existing rule, introducing exceptions and expanding or restricting its applicability.[136] Sadeghi adds the concept "legal inertia" to Jackson's previous work on "legal scaffolding". According to "legal inertia" laws would not change, unless social pressure would be strong enough to render a law intolerable or highly undesirable.[137]

Ibrahim expands on what was said by Jackson and Sadeghi, and focuses on the themes of flexibility and stability regarding the *ijtihād* and *taqlīd* dichotomy. Instead of understanding the relationship between *ijtihād* and *taqlīd* as a binary or a dichotomy, he presents us with a novel and more nuanced understanding of different levels of *ijtihād* and *taqlīd*. As such, he views them as the two ends of a continuum, with *ijtihād* in its "absolute" (*muṭlaq*)/"independent" (*mustaqill*) form occupying one end and "imitation" (*taqlīd*) in its most strict sense occupying the other.[138] Between the two he identifies several grades of the two modes such as intra-school *ijtihād* or *tarjīḥ*. Whereas the latter only allowed the scholar to weigh different opinions of his own school against one another based on the strength of evidence, the former enables the scholar to directly engage the scriptural sources in order to come up with a ruling on an unprecedented case, however, in the confines of his school's methodological and substantive parameters.[139]

Johansen's study demonstrates how new legal doctrines after the tenth century are introduced through the commentaries (*shurūḥ,* sg. *sharḥ*), legal responsa (*fatāwā*), and treatises on particular questions (*rasā'il*), while simultaneously the views of the early

---

[136] Ibid., p. 97 and 99.

[137] Behnam Sadeghi, *The Logic of Law Making in Islam: Women and Prayer in the Legal Tradition* (Cambridge: Cambridge University Press, 2013), p. xii-xiii, preface and see chapter 1. Both concepts, "legal scaffolding" and "legal inertia" are articulated by the legal historian Alan Watson.

[138] Ibrahim, "Rethinking the *Taqlīd* Hegemony: An Institutional, *Longue-Durée* Approach," p. 7-8.

[139] Ibid., p. 8-9.

school authorities are upheld in the *mutūn*, which are textbooks containing the dominant

school doctrine and served training purposes in the first place.[140]

Conclusion

The common theme of the critiques seems to be to point out that Islamic law in fact

continued to allow change even during the "*taqlīd* period". The above shows that the law

became not only more abstract and systematic, but at the same time it became almost like a

code, which provided more predictability and stability, new insights that run against many

assumptions orientalists had about Islamic law.[141]

However, all in all we can say that their scholarship with their important criticism

of orientalist scholars and their new insights does not really challenge the premises of the

dominant historiography. When they argue against orientalists that for example the law in

fact continued to evolve, then this evolution is still confined to the same framework of *fiqh*

that is found in the dominant historiography's scholarship. This becomes evident when we

assess their answers to questions regarding the legal actors, the legal sources to derive the

law, and the sources to study the history of Islamic law. We can observe that discussions

on *mazālim, ḥisba* and the role of non-jurists are not subsumed under the header

Sharia/Islamic law in their scholarship, as is the case in the dominant historiography of

Islamic law. Instead, we are presented with a narrative on jurists and works written by

jurists.

Despite their differences both scholarships keep Shalakany's premises One and

Two intact.[142] Therefore, I agree with Shalakany's characterization of the criticisms

---

[140] Baber Johansen, "Legal Literature and the Problem of Change," in *Contingency in a Sacred Law: Legal and Ethical Norms in the Muslim Fiqh*, ed. Baber Johansen. (Leiden: Brill, 1999), p. 447-448.

[141] Fadel, "State and the Sharia," p. 98.

[142] So far we only mentioned premise Two briefly, but we will deal with it in more detail in the following chapter.

levelled by the aforementioned revisionist scholars against the dominant historiography as "a refinement on the sharia/*siyāsa* dichotomy", which he calls "anti-Orientalist variations."[143] In essence, we are still left with a "binary" of a divine law on the one side and a "secular" law on the other side. The fundamental contribution of those "anti-Orientalist variations" should be seen in how they broaden our understanding of the Sharia/*fiqh* part. However, we are still left with a scriptural conception of Islamic law.[144]

Even if thanks to the very important contribution of scholars such as Hallaq, Jackson and others we have a more nuanced picture regarding the possibility and scope of legal change throughout the centuries of Islamic law, we are still left with the question regarding the role of the state in the lawmaking process and the state's relationship with jurists. In fact, Jackson and Ibrahim in particular discuss that relationship, as we will see in the next chapter (Chapter Three).

If we recall the strictly legal nature of the Sharia we talked about in chapter Two, then one of the characteristics of that designation was enforceable laws. This leads to the question of whether Islamic law was too rigid and too ideal to be enforced in real life. A number of scholars (particularly those belonging to the dominant historiography) hold such an opinion and characterized Islamic law as too ideal and too rigid. Therefore, they concluded that the ruling authorities couldn't rely on an unpractical Islamic law and were forced to circumvent it by creating their own secular parallel legal system, which in their view led to the existence of a dual legal system in the Islamic lands. That is the famous gap between theory and practice.

However, what is of particular importance here is to scrutinize the definition of what Islamic law is; who do we identify as legitimate legal actors in the legal-process,

---

[143] Shalakany, "Islamic Legal Histories," p. 60.
[144] Ibid.

especially in the area of law-making, what are the mechanisms of change, and who can initiate change and can Islamic law accommodate social change and respond to demands of society?

Dominant historiography tells us that Islamic law is a jurists' law. The role of the state is merely to implement and execute the laws of the jurists. In that endeavor the state is not envisaged to have any kind of discretion or participation in the lawmaking process. This understanding leaves us with the *fiqh* of the jurists from the four schools of jurisprudence as the "ideal" theory, which after the "closure of the gate of *ijtihad*" was not supposed to change anymore, which made it rigid as well as disconnected from reality. If this were the case, then it follows by default that there has been a gap between theory (law of the jurists in works of *fiqh*) and practice (law in action, as applied by the state). One could argue however, that this would not necessarily lead to gap, if the state only intervened in legal matters not covered by *fiqh*, which as we will see in the following chapter it did. We are expected to regard a theoretical discourse that dealt with a certain reality in the past as the "final" say on every legal matter yet to come.

The approach of such a narrative is very problematic as it, according to Ergene and Stilt, reduces the issue of the relationship between theory and practice to a simple question that seeks a yes or no answer, whether a doctrinal rule found in the treatises of jurists was applied in practice or not.[145] Stilt justifies this assessment by quoting Schacht who writes that the correspondence between the "ideal theory" of Sharia and practice was the "strongest on the law of family (marriage, divorce, maintenance, &c.), of inheritance, and of pious foundations (*wakf*); it was weakest, and in some respects even non-existent, on penal law, taxation, constitutional law, and the law of war; and the law of contracts and

---

[145] Boğaç Ergene, "Islamic Law in Action: A Historical Discussion," *Law & Social Inquiry* 38 (2013): p. 1046; Stilt, *Islamic Law in Action*, p. 1.

obligations stands in the middle."[146]

Accordingly, every practice that does not correspond to the letter of the law as expounded in the writings of jurists, is a deviation from the "ideal theory". This was, according to Schacht and Coulson, especially true for the realm of criminal law, due to the very strict requirements of evidence and proof. As a result, they argued, that rulers had to create their parallel and more effective legal system. We have to bear in mind that Schacht and Coulson regard jurists and their *fiqh* to be the only legitimate manifestation of the Sharia. This conception of Sharia, coupled with the claim that the Sharia reached its "final mould" in the early Abbasid period[147] or in the tenth century[148], assumes as Rohe argues, that only "early and classical developments [are viewed] as 'Islam' per se, while modern developments are considered as not being part of 'genuine' Islam and are consequently dismissed."[149] Additionally, this understanding dismisses the very possibility to evolve in regards to Islamic law.[150]

Ahmad Atif criticizes this very approach of scholars of Islamic law, who look for a "perfect consistency" of theory and practice in premodern Islamic law, which according to Atif is an ideal that cannot be encountered in any legal system. Instead, he proposes to study the structural interrelations between theoretical and practical reasoning.[151]

If one acknowledges that law plays in a social context and that law is constantly evolving, and that practice can influence theory, then it is not valid to approach the

---

[146] Schacht, *An Introduction to Islamic Law*, p. 76, cited in Stilt, *Islamic Law in Action*, p. 1, footnote 3.

[147] Schacht, *An Introduction to Islamic Law*, p. 75.

[148] Coulson, *A History of Islamic Law*, p. 5.

[149] Rohe, *Islamic Law in Past and Present*, p. 6.

[150] The ever-growing gap between theory and practice perceived by Schacht is unavoidable based on his understanding of Islamic law. Schacht says that Islamic law was only "adaptable and growing" up to the early Abbasid period and "from then onwards became increasingly rigid and set in its final mould." See Schacht, *An Introduction to Islamic Law*, p. 75; Coulson also argues that in "the tenth century the law was cast in a rigid mould from which it did not really emerge until the twentieth century." See Coulson, *A History of Islamic Law*, p. 5.

[151] Ahmad Atif Ahmad, *Structural Interrelations of Theory and Practice in Islamic Law: A Study of Six Works of Medieval Islamic Jurisprudence* (Leiden: Brill, 2006), p. xviii-xix in the Prologue.

question whether a gap between theory and practice existed in the history of Islamic law, by contrasting an "ideal theory" that reached its "final mould" and is denied to evolve, with an ever changing world.[152] Otherwise, any action and acts of discretion on account of the ruler, judges and non-jurists in the legal sphere that do not correspond to the "ideal theory", cannot be subsumed under Sharia and contribute towards the gap between theory and practice. In chapter Three we want to further problematize these points by including legal actors other than jurists into our discussion.

But, before we delve in to the topic of *siyāsa*, which will be the subject of the next chapter, we want to have a look at the most important points on Islamic criminal law and regulations of evidence and procedure as is found in the *fiqh* compendia of jurists.

Criminal Law According to *fiqh*

In the pre-modern legal works of Islamic jurists, we find a tripartition of criminal law in *qiṣāṣ, ḥudūd* and *taʿzīr*. The first, *qiṣāṣ*, deals with homicide and bodily injuries. The second category, the *ḥudūd*, involves those crimes which are mentioned in the Koranic text and the last category, *taʿzīr*, includes any other crimes that do not fall within the other two categories.[153]

Qiṣāṣ can be understood as *lex taliones* (talion law) and is derived from the Koranic verses 2:178-179.[154] It applies in instances of intentional killing and physical injury. It has a retaliatory function that allows the harmed party *(ʿāqila)* or the legal successor of the victim *(awliyāʾ al-dam)* to ask for retaliation, which entails the death penalty for the

---

[152] Rohe rightly argues that "limiting oneself to texts of abstract norms without reference to pre-legal conditions or attendant circumstances would result in a distorted image of any legal system." See Rohe, *Islamic Law in Past and Present*, p. 5.

[153] Rohe, *Islamic Law in Past and Present*, p. 155.

[154] „O ye who believe! Retaliation is prescribed for you in the matter of the murdered; the freeman for the freeman, and the slave for the slave, and the female for the female. And for him who is forgiven somewhat by his (injured) brother, prosecution according to usage and payment unto him in kindness. This is an alleviation and a mercy from your Lord. He who transgresseth after this will have a painful doom. And there is life for you in retaliation, O men of understanding, that ye may ward off (evil)." Verses quoted from the Koran translation *"The Meaning of the Glorious Koran"* by Marmaduke William Pickthall.

murderer in the case of premeditated homicide or the affliction of the proportionate amount

of damage in the case of intentional bodily harm. Aside from opting for corporeal

punishment, the party of the victim has the choice to ask for blood money *(diyya)*.[155] A

third choice would be to forgive and pardon *('afū)* the killer.[156] As Rohe points out, this

penal system assumes a social order with reliance on an extended family such as a tribe,

where any other form of further social security is not given.[157]

The *ḥudūd* (boundaries) crimes are called prescribed punishments, because they are

primarily fixed and based on Koranic texts, even though some important elements of those

punishments rely on the Sunna as well. These offenses are the following: highway robbery

(qaṭ' al-ṭarīq/ ḥirāba), theft *(sariqa)*, premarital illicit sexual relations *(zinā)*, wrongful

accusation of adultery *(qadhf)* and drinking of alcohol *(shurb al-khamr)*. Usually two

further offenses are categorized as prescribed punishments as well, which are apostasy

from Islam *(ridda)* and rebellion.[158]

Each offense requires the fulfillment of specific elements and if it is not possible to

meet those strict requirements, this does not mean that there will not be any sanction.

Regarding the case, the offence at hand could be tried under the less strict requirements of

ta'zīr, which is less fixed and allows for vast judicial discretion.[159] In addition to that, this

category also deals with every other crime that does not fall in the scope of the prescribed

offenses or the talion law. As mentioned above, discretionary punishment also applies, if

the certain elements of prescribed punishments are not met. As for example in the case of

the prescribed punishment for theft.[160] The prescribed punishment for theft is fixed by the

---

[155] Ibid. p. 179.

[156] Rudolph Peters, *Crime and Punishment in Islamic Law: Theory and Practice from the Sixteenth to the Twenty-First Century* (Cambridge: Cambridge University Press, 2005), p. 44.

[157] Rohe, Islamic Law in Past and Present, p. 179.

[158] Ibid. p. 156.

[159] Ibid. p. 185.

[160] Ibid. p. 177.

Koran chapter five verse 38, according to which the hand of the thief should be cut off.

However, the verse does not specify what exactly counts as theft. The constitutive factors

of this offense are expounded by jurists, who restricted the scope of this punishment by, for

example, defining that what was stolen has to be of a certain value *(niṣāb)*. Everything that

is lesser than this certain value cannot be subject to the prescribed punishment for theft, but

falls under the scope of judicial discretion.[161] This is very important to keep in mind,

because as we will see, *ta'zīr* was the entry point for the discretion of the ruler and his

agents.[162]

Evidence and Procedure According to *fiqh*

Regarding criminal procedure there are two important ends of spectrum that have to be

taken into account. On the one hand, it has to be assured that there are mechanisms, which

minimize the possibility of unjust and arbitrary convictions. On the other hand, the social

interest in the detection and the prevention of crimes has to be considered, which can lead

to the limitation of procedural safeguards, in order to facilitate prosecution and conviction

of criminals. In the Koran and Sunna, we do not find prescriptions regarding this dilemma.

Here, the discretion of the ruler is sought-after, which manifests itself in *siyāsa* (see

Chapter Three).[163]

Now we will look at what legal compendia of jurists have to say about evidence and

procedure. First of all, it is important to know that the "presumption of innocence" is also

true under Islamic law and only irrefutable evidence presented to judicial authorities can

prove that a punishable crime has been committed.[164] Also, the judgment of the judge

---

[161] Ibid. p. 162.

[162] Peters, *Crime and Punishment in Islamic Law*, p. 65-66.

[163] Matthew Lippman, Sean McConville and Mordechai Yerushalmi, *Islamic Criminal Law and Procedure: An Introduction* (Conneticut: Greenwood Press, Inc., 1988), p. 59.

[164] Mohamed Selim El-Awa, "Confession and Other Methods of Evidence in Islamic Procedural Jurisprudence," in *Criminal Justice in Islam: Judicial Procedure in the Shari'a*, ed. Muhammad Abdel Haleem et al. (London: I.B. Tauris,

(*qāḍī*) in *sharī'a*-courts has to rest on the information provided during the process, he

cannot base his verdict on his own knowledge or observations.[165] In short it can be said that

the main kinds of accepted evidence according to jurists are:

> "a confession (iqrār) of admission of guilt on the part of the criminal, and the
>
> statements of witnesses (bayyina), who should be two upright Muslim persons, who are
>
> intimately aware of the happenings or events to which they are bearing witness."[166]

Additionally, pronouncing an oath and the refusal of an oath by one or the other

party is accepted as evidence as well.[167] It stands out that in all three forms of proofs one

has to trust the spoken word of the involved parties, over anything else. But, as we will see,

jurists were not of the opinion that it is the words alone that constitute truth, rather they

were aware that speech is an ambiguous act. Therefore, in order to ascertain whether a

spoken word is true or wrong, jurists relied on external factors that would tip the "balance

in favor of one or the other."[168] In the case of confession it is a person's voluntary

determination to acknowledge his wrong-doing that acts as an external factor. Concerning

testimony, the external factor that makes the witness credible is his scrutinized social and

religious reputation, before he is admitted in front of the court. The refusal of taking an

oath in of itself is an external factor that sheds doubt on the respective individual's

assertions.[169] Despite all of that, jurists remained sceptic towards the ability of the judge to

discern true from false statements. Although, they argued that the "word" of neither party

---

2003), p. 115.

[165] Baber Johansen, "Signs as Evidence: The Doctrine of Ibn Taymiyya (1263-1328) and Ibn Qayyim al-Jawziyya (d. 1351) on Proof," *Islamic Law and Society* 9 (2002): p. 170. Regarding the knowledge of the judge see id. 175-176. While *ḥanafī* and *shāfi'ī* jurists accept the knowledge of the *qāḍī* as a type of proof, except in cases that fall under the category of *ḥuqūq Allāh*, jurists of the *mālikī* and *ḥanbalī* school of law do not regard the knowledge of the judge as proof at all.

[166] Selim El-Awa, "Confession and Other Methods of Evidence in Islamic Procedural Jurisprudence," p. 111.

[167] For different kinds of oaths, such as *li'ān* (mututal imprecation) or *qasāma*, see Baber Johansen, "Signs as Evidence: The Doctrine of Ibn Taymiyya (1263-1328) and Ibn Qayyim al-Jawziyya (d. 1351) on Proof," *Islamic Law and Society* 9 (2002): 168-193. Particularly p.171-173.

[168] Johansen, "Signs as Evidence," p. 169.

[169] Ibid.

can ever be regarded as "indisputable and certain knowledge" *('ilm yaqīn)*, they still had to allow such forms of proof, because the religious scripture displays their validity as proofs.[170]

Among all of these different forms of evidence, confession by the perpetrator of a crime is viewed as the highest degree in terms of establishing proof.[171] Thereby it is required that a given confession has to be detailed enough and the confessor has to prove that he is aware of the crime he committed. Furthermore, it is incumbent upon the judge to ask the confessor about particulars regarding the confessed crime, in order to avoid unjust punishment.[172] In cases of criminal law, such as the prescribed punishments *(hudūd)*, it is possible to retract one's confession during any stage of the process, be it before or after the judgment, or even during the actual execution of the punishment.[173] Regarding the validity or invalidity of a forced confession, we find different opinions. While the majority position stresses that a confession must be voluntarily and not acquired through force, the *hanbalī* and the *hanafī* schools of jurisprudence offer different views on the invalidity of forced confessions.[174] Johansen tells us that all of the four schools of jurisprudence regarded judicial torture not only as unreliable, but also as an illegitimate way to establish the "truth of facts"[175] and even characterized such practice as "sinful and criminal destruction of the trustworthiness of utterances", utterances that constituted the basis of the *qāḍī's* judgment.[176] As an exception, the *mālikī* school makes the application of torture dependent on the reputation of the defendant.[177]

---

[170] Ibid., p. 170.
[171] Selim El-Awa, "Confession and Other Methods of Evidence in Islamic Procedural Jurisprudence," p. 112.
[172] Ibid., p. 114.
[173] Rohe, *Islamic Law in Past and Present*, p. 160.
[174] Selim El-Awa, "Confession and Other Methods of Evidence in Islamic Procedural Jurisprudence," p. 116.
[175] Johansen, "Signs as Evidence," p. 170.
[176] Ibid., p. 171.
[177] Ibid., p. 170.

However, ultimately it can be said that it is up to the evaluation of the judge to either accept any kind of confession or rule against its admissibility, and it is also up to his discretion to accept or reject a retraction by the confessor.[178]

The second important mean of proof and evidence according to jurist's treatises is the testimony of witnesses. In their discussions jurists set very high requirements on the integrity of witnesses, whom they require to be honest and upright (*'adāla*). The testimony of people who fail to meet those strict qualifications and whose propriety is even slightly questionable, is to be rejected.[179] Among reasons which can render a person's testimony invalid is for example, whether that person has ever eaten in a public street. Jurists do also disagree on how to assess the probity of a witness and whether it is the duty of the judge to actively establish the integrity of a witness or to assume his probity if the contrary is not proven.[180] Since the end of the eighth century judges had a special assistant called *muzakkī* ("purifier"), whose job it was to assess the social and religious standing of witnesses and to establish whether they are "just witnesses" (*'udūl*). Those qualified by the *muzakkī* as such, would be registered as trustworthy witnesses, which rendered their testimony as acceptable court evidence.[181]

Generally, the testimony of two trustworthy witnesses is sufficient, however, there are exceptions to this rule, as is the case in proving adultery. The requirement for four witnesses stems from the Koran verse 15 in chapter 4, and verses 4 and 13 in chapter 24.[182] To be even more precise, in the case of adultery the testimony of four adult sane men is required. In *ḥudūd*-crimes the testimony of women was not accepted throughout the four

---

[178] Selim El-Awa, "Confession and Other Methods of Evidence in Islamic Procedural Jurisprudence," p. 116-117.

[179] Ibid., p. 117.

[180] Ibid., p. 119; Hina Azam, *Sexual Violation in Islamic Law: Substance, Evidence, and Procedure* (New York: Cambridge University Press, 2015), p. 191.

[181] Johansen, "Signs as Evidence," p. 171.

[182] Selim El-Awa, "Confession and Other Methods of Evidence in Islamic Procedural Jurisprudence," p. 120; Azam, *Sexual Violation in Islamic Law*, p. 188.

schools of jurisprudence. In addition, the specifics provided in the testimony of the four male witnesses describing one and the same sex act have to match one and another.[183] The witnesses who have to appear together in front of the judge have to agree in their testimony concerning the identity of the perpetrators, the nature of the sex act, and the place and the time it took place. Aside from those who do not meet the requirements of an honest and upright person, in addition, blind people, slaves and close family members of the parties involved were excluded as potential witnesses as well. As a result, the requirements in number, gender and character made it very unlikely, if not impossible, to convict a person for committing adultery.[184] One should also consider that even if four such witnesses were to be found, there is still the risk for them to become liable to the punishment for accusation of adultery (*qadhf*) in case their testimony does not converge on all major points, but rather conflict one another, or one of them would retract his testimony.[185]

In *ḥudūd*-cases in general, and *zinā*-cases in particular, a very important procedural principle encouraged the judge to find defects and shortcomings in the testimony of witnesses when interrogating them, in order to avert the punishment. This is done in accordance with the doubt maxim.[186] This maxim commanded judges to avoid punishments in cases of doubt and this was a mainstay of Islamic criminal law.[187] It is also interesting to point out that even though the *ḥanafī* school of jurisprudence regarded serving as a witness to be an act of virtue, they made an exception for the case of *ḥudūd*, because they saw it as preferable to conceal the moral misbehavior of others, instead of revealing them. An exception in that regard is only the case of theft (*sariqa*). While

---

[183] Azam, *Sexual Violation in Islamic Law*, p. 188-189. Regarding the reasoning for the exclusion of women testimony see id. p. 189.

[184] Ibid., p. 190-191.

[185] Ibid., p. 192-193.

[186] Ibid., p. 193-194.

[187] Intisar Rabb, *Doubt in Islamic Law: A History of Legal Maxims, Interpretation, and Islamic Criminal Law* (New York: Cambridge University Press, 2015), p. 4.

violations such as *zinā* infringe only rights of God (*ḥuqūq Allāh*), theft violates interpersonal rights (*ḥuqūq al-ʿibād*).[188] This also serves as a very interesting example in showing that Islamic Law's primary concern was in protecting rights of its subjects and preserving a just social order like any other legal system.

A further procedural obstacle in the case of *ḥudūd*-offences is the question regarding the right to petition (*daʿwā*), meaning who can bring forth charges against an offender. Here it is crucial whether the offense in question falls into the category of either divine rights, interpersonal rights, or both. Concerning violations of the second and last category, where a human is the victim, such as the breaking of contracts, or even *ḥudūd*-crimes such as theft and slander, the violated party has the right to petition, in order to seek redress. Regarding the violations of divine rights alone, a case is only heard if the perpetrators come forward themselves and confess what they did, or four witnesses that fulfill all of the above-mentioned requirements testify against them. The ruling authority is also allowed to bring forward charges in such cases.[189] However, one has to keep in mind the risks involved for witnesses and the severe punishment that would deter a person from incriminating himself.

All in all, Hina Azam rightly concludes that the guiding principle in scholarly discourse in the case of *zinā* is mercy and lenience, which motivated them to dismiss it and avoid the application of the *ḥudūd*-punishment at all cost. This is reflected in the high evidentiary standards and procedural principles that regulate the *ḥudūd* violations concerning the rights of God.[190] Because of God's sublime nature, he does not need his

---

[188] Azam, *Sexual Violation in Islamic Law*, p. 193-194.

[189] Ibid., p. 196-197.

[190] Ibid., p. 194. The high evidentiary requirements that were set in order to avoid the severe punishment for fornication that was conceptualized as a deterrent only can be seen as a double-edged sword, since at the same time that it protected consensual participants of sexual intercourse, the subsumption of coerced sex under *ḥadd* rendered a persecution of rapists almost impossible.

The *mālikī's*, however, classified rape as a composite crime, meaning as both *zinā*, but also as a form of property usurpation

rights and his claims to be satisfied, and moreover, the harsh *ḥudūd*-punishments are first and foremost conceptualized as a deterrent (*zajr*) and not "intended" to be applied.[191]

The above-mentioned points and sources are all in regards to the *fiqh* literature, which is the product of the jurists' endeavor and represents the substantive law that was applied in the Sharia-courts. According to Schacht and Coulson Islamic law (*fiqh*) was silent on some fields of the law or was not maturely developed in some aspects of the law, such as criminal law, criminal procedural law or administrative law. Moreover, Islamic criminal law as reflected in *fiqh* manuals does not make provisions for the use of circumstantial evidence[192] which renders any kind of criminal investigation almost impossible. In order to know how jurists and the state dealt with these difficulties, one has to look at *siyāsa* (Chapter Three).

However, the works of Johansen and Azam cast some doubt on Schacht's and Coulson's assessment of the inadmissibility of circumstantial evidence in *fiqh* generally and even in criminal proceedings in particular, by showing how for example architectural elements, expert opinion, the market price of goods, and pregnancy of an unmarried women was accepted as circumstantial evidence.[193]

It is true that the chapters on criminal law in *fiqh* works are very slim in comparison to other topics, such as rituals. As outlined above, criminal law in *fiqh* books is divided into *qiṣāṣ, ḥudūd* and *ta'zīr*. We have seen that the first two kinds are regulated very strictly and in great detail on the basis of scriptural indicants. It is also true that according to the evidentiary and procedural requirements of the two, the persecution of a number of

---

(*ightiṣāb*). They analogized female sexuality to property and accepted circumstantial evidence, which enabled victims of rape cases to "effectively" charge their assailants.

[191] Peters, *Crime and Punishment in Islamic Law*, p. 55.

[192] Schacht, *An Introduction to Islamic Law*, p. 192-193; Coulson, *A History of Islamic Law*, p. 125.

[193] Johansen, "Signs as Evidence," p. 173-175. See also Azam, *Sexual Violation in Islamic Law*, chapter 6, p. 201-238.

criminal offenses, such as theft and murder would be almost impossible. The third kind, however, leaves vast room for discretion and regulation, because of the lack of textual indicants. In that regard each category has its own evidentiary and procedural requirements, which are quite fixed in the first two, whereas they are almost non-existent for the last category, *ta'zīr*.[194] As such, *ta'zīr* was the entry gate for the ruler to regulate and influence legal proceedings substantially, by for instance allowing circumstantial evidence in criminal law.   In chapter Three we will deal with the status of circumstantial evidence in the context of "secular" legal institutions, outside of *fiqh* and the *qāḍī* court.

Conclusion

All in all, the narrative regarding the study of Islamic law put forward by Schacht and Coulson can be described as a narrative of legal compendia authored by jurists, or as Shalakany calls it, the "study of a corpus of black letter rules and standards."[195] In their view the study of Islamic law is the study of Sharia, and the normative legitimacy of the Sharia lies in its status of being the divine law of God that is embedded in his revelation to his messenger which is available for the jurists in form of scripture, the Koran and the Sunna. Jurists apply *uṣūl al-fiqh* in order to derive God's law from those sources, whereby aside from the scriptural sources Koran, Sunna and *ijmā'* the role of human reasoning is confined to analogical reasoning (*qiyās*), by which the jurist expands the application of rulings found in the sources to provide a solution for new cases. According to their history of Islamic law jurists debated during the "formative period" (632-850 CE) what the ideal form of 'Islamic jurisprudence' should look like. Following, around the 9th century, the famous scholar al-Shāfi'ī articulated his legal theory of *uṣūl al-fiqh* and his epistemological

---

194 Johansen, "Signs as Evidence," p. 176.
195 Shalakany, "Islamic Legal Histories," p. 15.

framework regarding valid legal sources and hermeneutics was "adopted" throughout the spectrum of the four schools of jurisprudence. From 950 up to 1798 CE the Sharia supposedly ossified due to the shift from *ijtihād* to *taqlīd*.[196]

This narrative is based on sources written by jurists from mainly the four schools of jurisprudence, such as legal compendia and collections of legal opinions from throughout the described three periods of the history of Islamic law. Shalakany writes that these kinds of juristic works "constitute the primary source materials for the field's dominant tradition in historiography [of Islamic law], and it is there that shari'a law can be discovered. It is therefore no surprise that both Schacht and Coulson regularly describe shari'a as an extreme case of pure "jurist law".[197] Therefore, the *fiqh*-literature constitutes what Islamic law really is.

As we have seen, Schacht and Coulson received serious backlash and a lot of their views, particularly those concerning the "closure of the gate of *ijtihād*", the role of al-Shāfiʿī and the relevance of secondary sources of legal theory were substantially nuanced and revised. Those scholars work off on the same sources used by Schacht and Coulson, adding to it the study of court records and a deep reading of different genres of legal literature that are connected with legal manuals, such as legal response (*fatāwā*), commentaries, glosses, super commentaries and biographical dictionaries.

However, one could question in how far their scholarship poses a challenge to Schacht's and Coulson's work, or whether it is possible to describe their valuable insights more as some kind of fine-tuning, modification or variation? The above-mentioned refinements do not really challenge the premises presented by Shalakany, instead they confine themselves to the framework for the study of the history of Islamic law put forward

---

[196] Ibid.
[197] Ibid., p. 15-16.

by Schacht and Coulson.[198] Because they agree that the Sharia is a body of rules and that it is jurists of the four legal schools who tell us what the norms of the Sharia are. We are still left with a story about jurists of the four schools of jurisprudence.

Furthermore, we have discussed the laws of evidence and procedure as expounded in *fiqh* manuals. Jurists conceptualized the *ḥudūd* crimes as a deterrent and tied the execution of their punishments to very high evidentiary and procedural requirements, such as the exclusion of circumstantial evidence, that made their prosecution almost impossible. Yet, *ḥudūd* crimes also include offenses such as theft that infringe both, the rights of god and the rights of man. Therefore, jurists made sure that if such a crime could not meet the high bars of *ḥudūd*, it could still be trialed under the discretionary proceedings of *taʿzīr*, which were less stringent (more on this in chapter Three). By doing so, jurists created a valve that allowed the state to safeguard the interests of the people through less strict evidentiary and procedural requirements, but at the same time to avoid the implementation of the very harsh punishments mentioned in scripture. The concept of rights of man and rights of God served as a very interesting justification in that regard.

In the case of the dominant historiography's narrative Islamic law stood in continuous tension with custom and the practice of political authorities, because Islamic law was perceived as too rigid, and thus it could not accommodate social change and was not practical for governance. This led to an ever-growing gap between theory and practice in Islamic law, with the result that it had to yield more and more of its jurisdiction to

---

[198] Although, Hallaq challenges Schacht on a number of issues, he conceptualizes the Sharia as a Law that is constructed by *madrasa* educated jurists. In his view the state had no influence in lawmaking until the nineteenth century. According to him the modern state and the Sharia are incompatible and thus, today the Sharia is not in practice anymore. For further information, refer to Hallaq, Wael B. "Can the *Shariʿa* be Restored." In *Islamic Law and the Challenges of Modernity*, edited by Yvonne Yazbeck Haddad and Barbara Freyer Stowasser, 21-53. Walnut Creek, CA: AltaMira Press, 2004; and Hallaq, Wael B. *The Impossible State: Islam, Politics, and Modernity's Predicament.* New York: Columbia University Press, 2013.

"secular" laws of the political authorities.

This leads us to the second premise of the dominant historiography described by Shalakany that exemplifies the inherent dichotomy of the dominant stream of scholarship, according to which the sacred and religious Sharia represents the binary opposite of the "secular" *siyāsa*. The second premise says that "the history of Islamic law is not the history of *siyāsa*."[199]

CHAPTER THREE

The following chapter deals with the relationship between religion and state in Islamic political theory with the focus on the role of the ruler and government. Especially the question of legal authority is of great importance in this regard. Throughout Islamic history legal authority underwent changes in regard to who held legal authority, who is creating law, who is executing law etc. Islamic society started with the Prophet as its leader and by time the Muslim society expanded very fast and not only society, but also the state grew more complex, diverse and was subject to different kinds of influences of the conquered regions, where they found a rich Roman and Persian tradition. Since society and regions changed and Muslims faced challenges on which the revealed text was silent, they had to find new ways to solve these problems, but at the same time to preserve their new religious identity. The concept of *siyāsa* played a very substantial role in this matter. However, what is *siyāsa* and in what kind of relationship does it stand to Islamic law? Is *siyāsa* Islamic or not and is it part of the normative Islamic framework or not? While some argue *siyāsa* was used in order to circumvent the inefficacy of Islamic law, others counter this claim by saying that *siyāsa* was used to supplement Islamic law.

---

[199] Shalakany, "Islamic Legal Histories," p. 16.

Religious and Political Authority in Early Islamic History

The time period of the prophet and the four rightly guided caliphs, which encompasses Abū Bakr (d. 634 CE), 'Umar ibn al-Khaṭṭāb (d. 644 CE), 'Uthmān ibn 'Affān (d. 656 CE) and 'Alī ibn Abī Ṭālib (d. 661 CE), is understood as a golden age and bears a normative character for Sunni Muslims, inter alia, in terms of governance.[200] The prophet and the four rightly guided caliphs embodied both religious and secular authority at the same time and there was no split between these two sources as in the later period of Islam.

The four rightly guided caliphs exercised comprehensive legal authority and they took legal actions which show little concern for the technicalities of the later established *fiqh*. Since the early Sharia legitimacy was based in the office of the caliph, their discretion in the application of the Sharia was non-negotiable.[201]

The Umayyad Period

Under the Umayyads, the caliphate was passed from the ruler to his son and that's why their critics accused them of having transformed the caliphate into kingship (*mulk*).[202] Furthermore, the Umayyad caliphs began to use the title "caliph of God" and saw themselves as divinely appointed deputies of God, as well as of the Messenger of God.[203] However, Umayyads often followed pre-Islamic customary law instead of implementing specific Islamic rules and law was developed through the practice of agents of the state such as judges, who were not trained in Islamic legal scholarship and relied to a huge extent on a combination of local custom, personal reasoning, ethical Koranic norms and

---

[200] W. Montgomery Watt, *Islamic Political Thought: The Basic Concepts* (Edinburgh: Edinburgh University Press, 1968), p. 36.

[201] Clifford E. Bosworth, Ian Netton, and Frank E. Vogel, "Siyāsa," in *Encyclopedia of Islam*, ed. by P. Bearman, Th. Bianquis, et al. (Leiden: Brill Online, 2010).

[202] Watt, *Islamic Political Thought: The Basic Concepts*, p. 38-39.

[203] Antony Black, *The History of Islamic Political Thought: From the Prophet to the Present* (New York: Routledge, 2001), p. 18.

elements derived from legal systems of the immediate geographical areas.[204]

However, the Umayyad caliphs were not recognized as rightly guided caliphs and their behavior did not have the normative character as the practice of their predecessors, the prophet and the four rightly guided caliphs had. They were viewed as kings and therefore we can talk about a split that took place between religious authority and worldly authority. Through military force the Umayyads became the de facto worldly rulers in the Muslim territories.

The Abbasid Period

In the year 750 CE the Abbasid revolution took place, which put an end to the Umayyad era. The Abbasids were the second Muslim dynastic monarchy and their empire lasted from 750-1258 CE. Abbasid rulers saw themselves as divine deputies of God and successors of the prophet. The deputy was supposed to hold religious and worldly authority in his hands, however, concerning the religious sphere they did not claim a monopoly. This was to be understood as executive power and not legislative.[205]

Instead, it was the Islamic jurists and scholars who possessed legislative authority in the religious field, which represented an essential element of the Abbasid rule in order to distinguish themselves from their Umayyad predecessors. However, the ruler had great freedom regarding administrative matters and created a judiciary aside from the *qāḍī* courts, which was more or less independent of the traditional jurists and their *fiqh* works. The institution of the market inspector *(muḥtasib)* and the *maẓālim* courts can be subsumed under this judiciary. Furthermore, criminal jurisdiction was mainly under the police

---

[204] Watt, *Islamic Political Thought: The Basic Concepts*, p. 65; Miriam Hoexter, "*Qāḍī, Muftī* and Ruler: Their Roles in the Development of Islamic Law," in Law, Custom, and Statute in the Muslim World: Studies in Honor of Aharon Layish, ed. Aharon Layish et al. (Leiden: Brill, 2007), p. 68.

[205] Black, *The History of Islamic Political Thought: From the Prophet to the Present*, p. 20-21.

(shurṭa). Even though the ruler could not modify the Sharia, he could influence its implementation by the appointment of judges and by defining which cases they could hear.[206]

According to the dominant historiography, this quasi "constitutional arrangement" was the result of the defeat of the state against the religious scholars during the *miḥna,* the Koranic inquisition that lasted from 833 CE to 848 CE. When in the Umayyad period judges and the rulers played a key role in shaping the law, from this point onwards this was now deemed to be the sole prerogative of scholars affiliated to one of the four Sunni schools of jurisprudence, who elaborated the law according to the hermeneutics of *uṣūl al-fiqh*. Therefore, one could say that in the realm of Islamic law scholars held legislative authority and the ruler and his agents held executive and judicial authority.[207]

A process of disintegration of the Abbasid caliphate started with the invasion of the Shiite Buyids in 945 CE. The Abbasid state shrank into a symbolic caliphate with no political control.[208] In 1055 CE Sunnite Turks ruled Baghdad as warlords and this marks the beginning of the Seljuq dynasty.[209] From this point on the Sultans held the power in their hand and they became the true rulers. They were legitimated by the caliph, who delegated authority on the Sultan.[210] This practice went on until Baghdad was destroyed by the Mongols and the last Abbasid caliph was killed in 1258 CE.[211] In 1260 CE the Mamluks defeated the Mongols, which made them the prevailing Sunni power of their time.[212] The decline of the caliphate in the 10th and 11th century CE promoted the rise of

---

[206] Watt, *Islamic Political Thought: The Basic Concepts*, p. 75-76.
[207] Hoexter, "*Qāḍī, Muftī* and Ruler: Their Roles in the Development of Islamic Law," p. 68; Ahmed Fekry Ibrahim, *Pragmatism in Islamic law: A Social and Intellectual History* (Syracuse: Syracuse University Press, 2015), p. 36.
[208] Black, *The History of Islamic Political Thought: From the Prophet to the Present*, p. 30.
[209] Watt, *Islamic Political Thought: The Basic Concepts*, p. 74.
[210] Black, *The History of Islamic Political Thought: From the Prophet to the Present*, p. 50-51.
[211] Ibid. p. 173.
[212] Ibid. p. 141.

military-caste sultans and thereby reinforced their outreach and engagement in *fiqh* and its institutions. This created a competition between the two legitimacies of *fiqh* and *siyāsa*.[213] Now we will have a closer look at the concept of *siyāsa*.

Siyāsa

In a broad sense *siyāsa* means any form of management.[214] In a specific sense it means the management of state affairs and public policy, where the ruler conducts the state affairs and manages his subjects. *Siyāsa* was especially relevant in the realm of public law, where the state is involved, such as criminal law. A further meaning in the political usage of the term *siyāsa* is the discretionary authority of the ruler and his agents, which according to some is exercised outside of the Sharia. Here, *siyāsa* can take on the meaning of punishment, which refers to the ruler's privilege to exercise violence in order to enforce his authority and preserve order.[215]

Brown quotes an incident from the life of the prophet that is found in Jalāl al-Dīn al-Dawānī's (d. 1512 CE)[216] treatise, in which he demonstrates an instance of discretion or "executive decision" on behalf of the Prophet. The report revolves around a dispute over water and one of the two parties, a man named Zubair b. al-ʿAwwām (d. 656 CE), comes to the Prophet to seek a solution from him, which he delivers. The man does not seem to be satisfied with the offered solution and alludes to the prophet that he ruled on behalf of the other party because he is his cousin. This upsets the prophet and prompts him to modify his decision by increasing the amount of water that he envisaged for his cousin.[217] Brown sees

---

[213] Bosworth, Netton, and Vogel, "Siyāsa."

[214] Abdessamed Belhaj, "Law and Order According to Ibn Taymiyya and Ibn Qayyim al-Jawziyya, A Re-Examination of *siyāsa shar'iyya*," in *Islamic Theology, Philosophy and Law, debating Ibn Taymiyya and Ibn Qayyim al-Jawziyya*, ed. Birgit Krawietz et al. (Berlin: De Gruyter, 2013), p. 401.

[215] Bosworth, Netton, and Vogel, "Siyāsa."

[216] Jalāl al-Dīn al-Dawānī (d. 1502) of Shiraz, was a *shāfiʿī* scholar and courtier of the Ak-Koyunlu dynasty, who wrote a treatise on *mazālim* courts, tribunal of wrongs and grievances.

[217] "Professor Jonathan Brown: Is there Justice Outside God's Law? SOAS University London," YouTube Video, 1:17:55, recorded lecture, posted by "SOAS University London" on 04.03.2016, min. 29:53-30:30.

this as an instance of "executive decision" on behalf of the prophet and compares his action to a modern judge giving a fine of contempt to a disrespectful party and al-Dawānī cites this report as a basis for the *maẓālim* court, where the prophet engages in *siyāsa* (as understood by him as *maẓālim/ jarā'im*), however, the word *siyāsa* was not used during the time of the prophet.[218]

The first occurrence of the term *siyāsa* falls in the reign of Muʿāwiya ibn Abī Sufyān (d. 680), the first Umayyad caliph and it does not carry the notion of being in contradiction with the Sharia. In the time of al-Māwardī (d. 1058) this is still the case and *siyāsa* along with the obligation to protect the religion is seen as the prerogative of the 'ideal caliph'.[219]

Yet, there are scholars who tried to set boundaries on the unlimited discretionary powers of the ruler and aimed to subordinate *siyāsa* to *fiqh*, which is apparent in the legal doctrine called *siyāsa shar'iyya*, which can be translated as governance in accordance with the Sharia.[220] One reason for the need to limit the discretionary powers of rulers could be seen in the abuse of those discretionary powers by head of states, such as Mongol rulers.

Starting with the Mongols destruction of Baghdad in 1258 CE and with them converting to Islam their legacy and that of their related dynasties became part of the

---

In his lecture, Brown speaks about the anxiety of a tension between the rule of law as dictated in scripture/scriptural manifestation/indications in scripture on one hand and notions of justice/equity on the other hand. This lecture is based on his forthcoming book "*Justifying Secular Justice: The Edited Text of Jalal al-Din Davani's Treatise on Mazalim Courts*" and was delivered at SOAS University of London on the 29th of February 2016. It is available to watch through the following links that were both last accessed on October 2nd 2016:

1. https://blogs.soas.ac.uk/muslimwise/2016/03/09/event-recording-is-there-justice-outside-gods-law-making-sense-of-the-boundaries-of-the-shariʿah-in-islamic-civilization-by-professor-jonathan-brown-alwaleed-bin-talal-chair-of-islamic-civi/
2. https://www.youtube.com/watch?v=e403Hn3L9CU

I am aware about the intricacies of using a visual internet source in a paper, however, the lecture is delivered by a professor from a reputable university (Georgetown University DC) in an academic venue at another famous institution (SOAS University London). Furthermore, the video does not seem to be edited.

[218] Ibid., min. 30:33-31:57.

[219] Ovamir Anjum, "Siyasa al-Sharʿiyya," In *Oxford Encyclopedia of Islam and Law*, edited by Jonathan Brown. (Oxford: Oxford University Press).
http://www.oxfordislamicstudies.com/article/opr/t349/e0077?_hi=0&_pos=1

[220] Clifford E. Bosworth, Ian Netton, and Frank E. Vogel, "Siyāsa," in *Encyclopedia of Islam*, ed. by P. Bearman, Th. Bianquis, et al. (Leiden: Brill Online, 2010).

Islamic world.[221] Brown describes this legacy as an alternative notion of legitimacy to rule

outside the scope of the Sharia, something which did not exist in the Muslim world prior to

the coming of the Mongols. For example, the Timurid and Muslim ruler Timur/Tamerlane

(d. 1405) ruled his empire by what is called *yāsa*.[222] This type of law involved very harsh

punishments for a number of crimes, all of which showed no concern for the formalities of

fiqh. Among others this included "capital punishment for people who lie, use magic,

nourish prisoners or urinate in standing water."[223] This could be seen as an abuse of *siyāsa*

by rulers. Some scholars from the Ayyūbid and Mamluk periods associate the *siyāsa* of

their time with discretionary punishments of the ruler, some of which they saw as "being

opposed" to Sharia. Other scholars, such as al-Maqrīzī (d. 1442) and Ibn Khaldūn (d. 1442)

even equated *siyāsa* with the above-mentioned Mongol law.[224]

Siyāsa shar'iyya started to evolve in the late medieval times and it revolves around

the reconciliation of the practical demands of governance on the one hand, which is *siyāsa*

and the law and procedures of Islamic jurisprudence that is found in the *fiqh* literature on

the other hand. The most famous and important representatives of this doctrine are Ibn

Taymiyya (d. 1328 CE) and his student Ibn Qayyim al-Jawziyya (d. 1350 CE).[225]

Siyāsa shar'iyya grants the ruler the right to take legal action, which entails

legislating in order to supplement the Sharia, if public welfare is concerned (*maṣlaḥa*

'āmma). There are different and competing understandings of *siyāsa shar'iyya* and

whereas some formulations only allow for this in cases where the Sharia does not provide a

text for, others stress that the ruler's *siyāsa shar'iyya* is not allowed to infringe the Sharia

---

[221] "Professor Jonathan Brown: Is there Justice Outside God's Law? SOAS University London," YouTube Video, min. 40:52-41:21.

[222] Ibid., min. 41:25-43:11. In the context of *yāsa* see also *töre* and *yargu*.

[223] Rohe, *Islamic Law in Past and Present*, p. 187.

[224] Anjum, "Siyasa al-Shar'iyya."

[225] Bosworth, Netton, and Vogel, "Siyāsa."

and others again discard the recourse to it whenever there is a ruling in the *fiqh* literature. More practical conceptions of *siyāsa shar'iyya* stipulate the requirement that it must not contradict indisputable tenets of the Sharia. A more practical approach demands only that it does not contradict the spirit of the Sharia and its principles.[226]

Even though, *siyāsa shar'iyya* as a concept was accepted throughout Islamic history, there was disagreement on its limits and restrictions, which were subject to an ongoing process of negotiation between the state and his agents on one side, and the community of religious scholars (*'ulamā'*) on the other side. Depending on the historical context scholars were more inclined to grant the state a greater amount of discretion and at other times they dismissed some of the state's actions as unislamic. Thus, we cannot talk about one correct manifestation of *siyāsa,* but instead we have to acknowledge that there are competing views of *siyāsa.*

According to Ibn Taymiyya the *siyāsa* rules of the ruler would not contradict with the *fiqh,* if the Sharia is properly observed. He denied the view of earlier scholars who deemed it legit that rulers were allowed to and sometimes even had the need to deviate from the *fiqh* for the sake of efficiency. In contrast to them he did not assume that there would be a conflict between both or that the ruler had to deviate from *fiqh.* However, if there is a perceived conflict then according to Ibn Taymiyya this is because of a too narrow understanding of *fiqh* and would thereby mean to disregard the diverse sources that are offered by the Sharia in order to attain the public good, or this conflict has to be attributed to the ruler's non-compliance with the divine law. If the latter is the case then Ibn Taymiyya terms it *siyāsa ẓālima,* an unjust act, which is not to be confused with the true *siyāsa (siyāsa 'ādila)* that his student Ibn Qayyim understood as part of the Sharia *(fa hiya*

---

[226] Bosworth, Netton, and Vogel, "Siyāsa."; Anjum, "Siyasa al-Shar'iyya."

min al-sharī'a)[227]. Ibn Taymiyya envisions that both the ruler and the religious scholars commonly uphold Islamic law including its form that is laid out in particular rulings and also its general principles and objectives.[228] In order to realize this vision, Ibn Taymiyya proposed a broader understanding of the above mentioned secondary sources, *maslaha* in particular. He argued for a notion of *maslaha* that goes beyond textual indications, or specific "interests" already mentioned in scripture. In contrast to that, *maslaha* could "encompass all acts, norms, and arrangements that are demanded by justice and public welfare, although they cannot contradict explicit and agreed-upon rules of the *Sharī'ah*."[229] This constitutes a more comprehensive picture of Sharia, one that does not conceptualize Sharia as the sole domain of the *'ulamā'* and norms of the four schools of jurisprudence, but rather as one that makes the ruler and his agents legitimate stakeholders by granting them some authority to partake in the process of shaping aspects of the Sharia.[230]

A number of very important legal institutions are legitimated under the doctrine of *siyāsa*, among which is the office of the *muhtasib*, the *qānūn* and special courts, such as the *mazālim* courts and the *jarā'im* courts.

Premise Two of the Dominant Historiography

As we have shown above, Schacht views Islamic law as a jurists' law developed by religious scholars that is only reflected in the *fiqh* literature[231], "not law as it was applied by courts, followed in customary practices, or administered and enforced by state representatives."[232]

---

[227] Ibn Qayyim al-Jawziyya, *al-Ṭuruq al-Ḥukmiyya fī al-Siyāsa al-Shar'iyya*, edit. Nā'if b. 'Aḥmad al-Ḥamad (Mecca: Dār 'Ālam al-Fawā'id, 2007), p. 8.
[228] Bosworth, Netton, and Vogel, "Siyāsa."
[229] Anjum, "Siyasa al-Shar'iyya."
[230] Ibid.
[231] Schacht, *An Introduction to Islamic Law*, p. 5.
[232] Shalakany, "Islamic Legal Histories," p. 6.

Schacht also argues that due to its failure of accommodating the continuously changing demands of society and because of its ineffectiveness in proving crimes, Islamic law had to yield to custom and the practice of the political authorities.[233] This approach views Islamic law as scriptural and textual only, which means that all extra textual factors such as the *maẓālim* courts, the office of the *muḥtasib*, the *qānūn*, everything that is legitimated under the *siyāsa* doctrine and instances of discretion in court practice will all fall outside of this understanding of Islamic law. As a result, such an understanding leaves us with a dichotomy between the "secular" *siyāsa* of the state and the "ideal" "religious" Sharia of the jurists. An understanding that "characterize(d) the last century of thinking in the field (and can still be found fallaciously today)."[234] In the previous chapter (Chapter Two) we focused on the Sharia (*fiqh*) side of that dichotomy and now we want to look at the *siyāsa* side of it.

According to Schacht, Islamic law as found in *fiqh* books was the least developed or even almost absent in the areas of criminal law, taxation, and constitutional law, all of which belong to the realm of public law. Whereas the highest degree of agreement of both theory and practice is supposed to be found in the areas of personal status law and religious endowments.[235]

The *qāḍī/ sharī'a*-courts were required to apply the law provided by jurists, meaning the law found in the *fiqh*-works of the four schools of jurisprudence. Schacht says that based on the *fiqh* discourse the state authorities are left with very limited discretion and cannot rely on circumstantial evidence in criminal law, prosecution and

---

[233] Schacht, *An Introduction to Islamic Law*, p. 76-77.
[234] Rudolph Peters and Peri Bearman, ed., *The Ashgate Research Companion to Islamic Law* (Surrey: Ashgate Publishing Press, 2014), Preface.
[235] Shalakany, "Islamic Legal Histories," p. 16.

investigation.[236] The scriptural sources only mention eye witnesses, oaths, confession and denial as evidence. In order to remedy this ineffectiveness rulers took recourse to "secular" non-Islamic institutions that were Islamized; the *maẓālim* court and the office of the market inspector (*muḥtasib, ḥisba*).[237]

Schacht concedes that only "owing to the ambiguity"[238] of its meaning, *siyāsa* is acceptable under the "strict theory" of Islamic law. Furthermore, for Schacht *siyāsa* can only be of a very limited scope, meaning that the ruler just has the right to "make administrative regulations within the limits laid down by the sacred law."[239] This is in line with the "constitutional agreement" that denies the ruler any legislative function, which essentially means that although Schacht accepts the validity of a very limited *siyāsa* competence for the ruler and his agents, they were nevertheless denied to go beyond the legal doctrines of the four Sunni schools of law.

Siyāsa is mainly concerned with public law, such as penal law or taxation among others, all matters that involve the state to at least some degree. It is very interesting to note that Schacht's narrative informs us that particularly this sphere governed by *siyāsa*, was the area where the application of Islamic law was either "most lacking" or "even non-existent".[240]

We also see Schacht juxtaposing the "secular" administrative justice of the ruler

---

[236] Schacht remarks that the evidentiary rules of Islamic law "made it impossible for the *ḳāḍī* to undertake a criminal investigation, and his inability to deal with criminal cases became apparent. Consequently, the political powers stepped in and transferred the administration of the greater part of criminal justice to the police *(shurṭa)*, and it has normally remained outside the sphere of practical application of Islamic law." See p. 50 in Schacht, An Introduction to Islamic Law. See further id. p. 82, where Schacht writes: "We have seen that Islamic law, at a very early period, diverged both from an explicit ruling of the Koran and from current practice by denying the validity of documentary evidence and restricting legal proof to the oral evidence of witnesses." See also id. p. 192-193 where it says that "circumstantial evidence is not admitted."

[237] Shalakany, "Islamic Legal Histories," p. 18-19. For a detailed account on evidence and procedure in *fiqh* and a partial correction of Schacht's and Coulson's assumption regarding the absence of circumstantial evidence in *fiqh*, see chapter Two.

[238] Schacht, *An Introduction to Islamic Law*, p. 54.

[239] Ibid., p. 53.

[240] Shalakany, "Islamic Legal Histories," p. 17; Schacht, *An Introduction to Islamic Law*, p. 76.

and his agents in opposition to the ideal "religious" law applied by the *qāḍī*. In his view the institutions legislated under the rulers' *siyāsa* gradually took over competencies from the *qāḍī* courts, while he characterizes only the latter to exercise its duty based on the Sharia.[241]

Because *qāḍī* courts, applying "Islamic law in substance and procedure" were incapable to effectively deal with matters of criminal law and therefore, the political authorities took away most of criminal law jurisdiction from *qāḍī* courts. Which leads Schacht to the conclusion that Islamic criminal law "normally remained outside the sphere of practical application."[242]

Additionally, Schacht tells us that *Maẓālim* courts that were created "ostensibly" to supplement the *qāḍī* courts, instead encroached on the latter's jurisdiction. He cites those examples in order to substantiate his claim that Islamic law, inter alia the Sharia – which according to him is *fiqh* – was early on substituted by the political authorities.[243]

Along similar lines Schacht talks about how the *muhtasib* deprived the *qāḍī* courts from parts of their jurisdiction, while stressing that "the procedure of the *muhtasib* did not always satisfy the strict demands of Islamic law."[244]

In the view of dominant historiography rulers saw the need to circumvent the ideal, but unpractical Sharia courts, in order to implement effective and practical sets of rules, which they realized through the creation of alternative courts and the office of the market inspector. Orientalists see these *maẓālim* courts as secular ones in contrast to the religious and ineffective Sharia courts. Although Muslim jurists elaborated on *maẓālim* courts and the fact that they considered them to be legitimate, orientalists assess this acceptance as a

---

[241] Schacht, *An Introduction to Islamic Law*, p. 54.
[242] Ibid., p. 50.
[243] Ibid., p. 51.
[244] Ibid., p. 52.

surrender to secular absolutism. In addition to that they also regard the concept of *siyāsa shar'iyya*, which granted the ruler the right to make rules and regulations that are in accordance with Islamic law, as being un-Islamic. They attributed this to the fact that unlike Islamic law that is reflected in the *fiqh* literature and is rooted in revelation, *siyāsa shar'iyya* and the legislation of the ruler is not. Thereby it cannot be regarded as legitimate legislation, because according to Islam God is the solely legitimate legislator. Orientalists understand the existence of this concept, where Muslim jurists concede legislation to a ruler as a confirmation of their assumption that governing on the basis of revealed law whose text was frozen in time was infeasible. It had to be impossible to such an extent that even jurists acknowledged this fact and had no choice other than authorizing the secular ruler.[245]

In addition, one has to consider the quasi "constitutional agreement" between the ruler and the jurists, according to which the latter provided the laws to be followed in courts and the former was expected to execute the laws of the latter. Any discrepancy between the law in the books of *fiqh*, authored by jurists, and the law applied in the courts, or any other legal institution that is more or less independent of *fiqh*, must be a deviation from Sharia. The "deviant" legal institutions legislated by the ruler are characterized as secular in opposition to the religious law of the jurists. Those secular legal institutions are not produced by jurists and do not follow the ideal theory of *uṣūl al-fiqh*. The need for the state's special legal arrangements are seen as a failure of religious legal institutions. In that sense the dominant historiography does not understand *siyāsa* as a way to supplement the Sharia, but instead, as a mean to circumvent the Sharia.[246]

---

[245] Fadel, "State and the Sharia," p. 96; Shalakany, "Islamic Legal Histories," p. 18-19.

[246] This is not true for Coulson who held the opinion that the Sharia as law only constituted a part of the Islamic legal system, along extra Sharia jurisdictions that were admitted by necessity and not seen "as deviations from any ideal standard." See p. 134 and chapter Nine in Coulson, Noel J. *A History of Islamic Law*. Edinburgh: Edinburgh University

As a result, we are left with a dichotomy between a "religious" sphere on the one side and a "secular" sphere on the other side. This narrative tells us that the "religious" sphere, which equated with the Sharia was steadily losing its jurisdiction to the "secular" state, until it was finally replaced during the reform period of the 19th century. Now we want to examine, whether this is the only possible "plot" of Islamic law.

The Problem of Defining What the Sharia is

At the bottom of such a discrepancy, as described above, between legitimate Islamic law and "deviate, secular" manifestations of law in Islamic history, lies the question regarding what Sharia is. Let's recall our initial definition of Sharia, as "...the set of divine commands, transmitted by God through the foundational sources of Quran and Sunna, and *fiqh* is the human endeavor to identify and elucidate these divine injunctions."[247]

First of all, this definition tells us that the Sharia is a body of rules. Second, those rules are embedded in scripture. Third, *fiqh* is the science to derive this body of rules from scripture. Therefore, if we are told that jurists, educated in the science of *fiqh* engage scripture in their legal manuals, it would follow that we would consult their works of substantive law in order to know what the Sharia is, which also means that Sharia and *fiqh* is one and the same. This is the approach of the dominant historiography based on their interaction with juristic discourse, where a substantial number of Muslim jurists themselves present fiqh as Sharia in contrast to *siyāsa*. As a consequence, everything that is not found in the *fiqh*-literature cannot be subsumed under the label Sharia. Furthermore, the substantive laws of *fiqh* are seen as the *qāḍī's* law as applied in Sharia courts. If we equate Sharia with *fiqh*, then the assessment of the Sharia's application in practice is

---

Press, 1978.
[247] Peters and Bearman, "Introduction: The Nature of the Sharia," p. 1.

reduced to a simple yes or no question whether court practice corresponds to legal doctrines of *fiqh* or not. Further, it is understandable that if chapters on *maẓālim* courts, *jarā'im* courts, *ḥisba*, or *qānūn* are absent from works of *fiqh*, then of course those institutions could not be seen as legitimate manifestations of the Sharia. In order to better grasp the problem at hand, we will look at the following story.

Scholars in Mosul wrote to the founder of the Ayyubid dynasty, sultan Nūr al-Dīn Zankī (d. 1174) about a crime wave in the city that led to a number of murdered people. In their message they wrote that this issue requires some type of *siyāsa*, meaning the executive authority of the state.[248] In his response to the call of action from the scholars, the sultan said that he is not able to follow their request, arguing that if God had wanted in his Sharia to include a solution to the problem at hand, then he would have revealed it there, but since he chose not to do so, the sultan said that he will not intervene.[249]

Brown says that Nūr al-Dīn Zankī according to his understanding did not want to go against the law of God that did not seem to provide a solution for that particular problem.[250] He describes the event as a "crisis of justice". The scholars of Mosul argued that people have rights (*ḥuqūq*), such as rights to security, rights to property and right to public order. In the situation, they were experiencing in Mosul none of these rights were being preserved. When the Sultan denied their request, he was basically excluding those rights as a part of the law of God.[251]

According to the Sultan's understanding Sharia is the equivalent of scripture as it stands and the *fiqh* literature. This is a very similar understanding like the dominant

---

[248] "Professor Jonathan Brown: Is there Justice Outside God's Law? SOAS University London," YouTube Video, min. 8:47-9:51.

[249] Ibid., min. 10:17 – 10:36. We are not interested in the historicity of the events mentioned in this story, what concerns us here is the contrast between the different notions of what constitutes the divine law.

[250] Ibid., min. 10:47-10:56.

[251] Ibid., min. 12:37-13:08.

historiography's understanding. Did jurists really assume to solve all legal questions and deny the ruler or his agents to participate in the legal process? The answer is no, and in the following we will provide a number of examples to argue for a broader understanding of Sharia that goes beyond what is found in works of *fiqh*.

The notion that rulers of Muslim societies had created their secular parallel system of law that existed outside of the Sharia and was administered in the non-Sharia courts such as the *maẓālim* courts, is challenged by several scholars such as Jackson, Rapoport, Johansen, Shalakany etc. Through the work of medieval scholars like Ibn Taymiyya, Ibn Qayyim and other scholars they demonstrate that *siyāsa* was incorporated into Islamic law and thus *siyāsa* was normalized by jurists and became a legitimate mode of law from an Islamic perspective.

The doctrine of *siyāsa* shows us the importance of secondary sources of *uṣūl al-fiqh* in Islamic law, especially the two concepts *maṣlaha mursala* (general necessity and public benefit independent of scripture) and *sadd al-dharā'i'*. The concept of *maṣlaha mursala* in particular plays an important role in the *mālikī* and *ḥanbalī* discourse; they regarded every action (*'amal*) that is not harmful and that carries a benefit (*maṣlaha*) that outweighs its harm, as necessary (*maṭlūb*), without demanding any particular evidence (*shāhid*) for such a benefit. In his legal reasoning Mālik utilized *maṣlaha mursala* against scriptural texts by way of specification (*takhṣīṣ*) in the case of isolated reports *(khabar wāhid)* and ambiguous Koranic texts. According to the *ḥanbalī* school of jurisprudence the purpose of God's Sharia is to serve the benefit of his servants. The concept of *sadd al-dharā'i'* [252] is worth

---

[252] *Sadd al-dharā'i'* refers to the blocking of "the means to an expected end which is likely to materialise if the means towards it is not obstructed." Kamali further says "although the literal meaning of *sadd al-dhara'i'* might suggest otherwise, in its juridical application, the concept of *sadd al-dhara'i'* also extends to 'opening the means to beneficence'." But, generally the concept *sadd al-dharā'i'* is understood in the context of blocking the means that lead to evil, rather than opening the means that lead to benefit. A typical example for *sadd al-dharā'i'* would thus be "*khalwah* or illicit privacy between members of the opposite sexes", which "is unlawful because it constitutes a means to *zina* whether or not it actually leads to it." Mohammad Hashim Kamali, *Principles of Islamic Jurisprudence* (Cambridge:

mentioning when we talk about *maṣlaḥa mursala* in the context of the *ḥanbalī* school. Both

concepts assume the existence of universal benefits (*maṣāliḥ kulliyyā*) that are inherent in

scripture, although not articulated specifically in a particular text (*naṣṣ*). Furthermore, both

serve the same purpose, that is protecting the public good and repelling all kinds of

harm.[253] The *ḥanbalī's* also regard *sadd al-dharā 'i '* as the entry point of *siyāsa shar 'iyya*.

In accordance with *sadd al-dharā 'i '*, the ruler is authorized to prohibit things, that are

otherwise allowed and adopt unspecified measures that serve the public good. By blocking

the means that lead to harm and by opening the means that benefit the general community,

it is assured that the Sharia fulfills its purposes and intentions according to changing times

and places. Therefore, the above mentioned tools and concepts are promoted by scholars in

order to reconcile the Sharia with social change.[254]

However, scholars differ on the scope of the state's role in the legal sphere, whereas

some paint a picture that is closer to the separation of powers theory of the dominant

historiography, where the state only has executive authority, others started to provide a

picture in which the state is believed to have occupied a larger role in the area of

lawmaking. The scholarship of the former shows that the state could in fact influence the

legal outcome by different means, however, those means are still restricted to the content

of the jurists' *fiqh*. The state could for example set a canon of works to be studied in

madrasas and thereby influence the education of future judges and legal consults.

Furthermore, the ruler was able to appoint and dismiss judges, he could also obligate

---

Islamic Texts Society, 1991), p. 269.

[253] Birgit Krawietz, *Hierarchie der Rechtsquellen im Tradierten Sunnitischen Islam* (Berlin: Duncker & Humblot, 2002), p. 244-245.

[254] Krawietz, *Hierarchie der Rechtsquellen im Tradierten Sunnitischen Islam*, p. 274-276. See further p. 225, 235, and p. 244-245 in Opwis, *Maṣlaḥa and the Purpose of the Law*. Najm al-Dīn al-Ṭūfī (d. 1316 CE) for example has a very broad understanding of *maṣlaḥa mursala* and uses it as an argument not only in cases where the text is ambiguous or absent. Rather, he argues that a certain benefit should be the central criteria regulating every question outside of worship and rituals (*'ibāda*).

judges to follow certain legal opinions in some cases, in order to guarantee a specific legal outcome.[255]

The latter group views the state's legislative authority as an equal legitimate Islamic notion of law, as the *fiqh* expounded by jurists. In that sense, the state could supplement the law and it would be more appropriate to speak about more than one, sometimes even competing, articulations of Sharia. In such a narrative, the jurists do not have the monopoly to decide the content of the law, instead we could talk about different and sometimes even overlapping spheres.[256]

The main difference between the two groups is that the first group views the Sharia as a body of rules derived by scholars of the four schools of law, whereas the second group argues for a broader and more abstract definition of the Sharia that goes beyond norms articulated by jurists of the four legal schools, including among others "criminal justice measures of Mamluk princes, or the norms and structures of Ottoman political governance"[257], the "functionally-evolving *siyasa* courts"[258], the workings of the *muhtasib*, and considerations of equity and the spirit of the law in favor of the letter of the law.

Procedural Intervention and Structuring through the State

In terms of Islamic constitutional law Sherman Jackson offered a new approach through his

---

[255] See particularly Ibrahim, Ahmed Fekry. *Pragmatism in Islamic law: A Social and Intellectual History.* Syracuse: Syracuse University Press, 2015; Burak, Guy. *The Second Formation of Islamic Law: The Hanafi School in the Early Modern Ottoman Empire.* New York: Cambridge University Press, 2015; and Hoexter, Miriam. "*Qāḍī, Muftī* and Ruler: Their Roles in the Development of Islamic Law." In *Law, Custom, and Statute in the Muslim World: Studies in Honor of Aharon Layish,* edited by Aharon Layish and Ron Shaham, 67-85. Leiden: Brill, 2007.

[256] See particularly Rapoport, Yossef. "Royal Justice and Religious Law: *Siyāsah* and Shari'ah under the Mamluks." *Mamluk Studies Review* 16 (2012): 71–102; Stilt, Kristen. *Islamic Law in Action: Authority, Discretion, and Everyday Experiences in Mamluk Egypt.* New York: Oxford University Press, 2012; Johansen, Baber. "A Perfect Law in an Imperfect Society: Ibn Taymiyya's Concept of "Governance in the Name of the Sacred Law"." In *The Law Applied: Contextualizing the Islamic Shari'a: A Volume in Honor of Frank E. Vogel,* edited by Frank E. Vogel, Pear Bearman et al., 259-294. Leiden: I.B. Tauris, 2008; Ibid. "Signs as Evidence: The Doctrine of Ibn Taymiyya (1263-1328) and Ibn Qayyim al-Jawziyya (d. 1351) on Proof." *Islamic Law and Society* 9 (2002): 168–193; and Vogel, Frank E. *Islamic Law and Legal System: Studies of Saudi Arabia.* Leiden: Brill, 2000.

[257] Shalakany, "Islamic Legal Histories," p. 6.

[258] Ibid., p. 62.

analysis of the work of Shihāb al-Dīn al-Qarāfī (d. 1258 CE), where the premodern Islamic scholar analyses different functions of the prophet. This is Jackson's starting point for a constitutional approach to the interpretation of Islamic law.[259] Al-Qarāfī argues that the prophet acted in different capacities, for instance as a prophet, a mufti, a judge, or as a leader of a state. These capacities were inherited by different key players of the Muslim community. Therefore, it is of utmost importance to determine the function in which he acted in each precedent, in order to fully understand and apply it.[260] According to this view Muhammad acted in his capacity as a prophet whenever he was conveying the revelation and as a *muftī*, when he was drawing obligations and rules out of it. The function of communicating revelation was inherited by Koran reciters and Hadith transmitters. The *muftī* inherited the prophet's function of interpreting the texts, but whereas the prophet was infallible, the *muftī* is not and therefore his interpretation is not binding. When the prophet functioned as a judge this means that the right in question could only be exercised once it was authorized by a judge. This capacity was inherited by judges, who are concerned with the resolution of disputes and they rely on evidence such as eyewitness testimony, confessions and oaths. Whenever the prophet made a decision as the head of state, then these rulings do not represent general legal norms, but rather decisions made by the temporal ruler of the state. Depending on the assessment for the communities' welfare, these decisions could therefore be followed by rulers of the Muslim communities, or modified, or even ignored. Rulers of Muslim communities, whether they are caliphs, sultans or kings, etc., inherited this function of the prophet and are the head of the community in their lifetime, during which they own the authority of making binding

---

[259] Fadel, "State and the Sharia," p. 98. See Jackson, Sherman. "From Prophetic Actions to Constitutional Theory: A Novel Chapter in Medieval Muslim Jurisprudence." *International Journal of Middle East Studies* 25 (1993): 71–90.

[260] Sherman Jackson, "From Prophetic Actions to Constitutional Theory: A Novel Chapter in Medieval Muslim Jurisprudence," *International Journal of Middle East Studies* 25 (1993): p.74.

decisions for the sake of the community. Based on that, the following constitutional system can be expressed: The decisions of the judges are final under the condition that it is in accordance with the rules of law laid out by the *muftī*. The four schools of jurisprudence whose rules constituted the basis for the courts, enjoy quasi-constitutional status. The ruler is responsible for directing the public affairs of the community. In addition to that he has the right to act as a quasi-mufti to give legal opinions and resolve disputes like a judge. However, he has to rely on the opinions of the legal schools and is not allowed to interfere in the autonomous process of law-making or to interfere in the integrity of its application. Al-Qarāfī's theory seems to grant the ruler enormous legal and judicial power, but at the same time the fact that these powers of the ruler are confined by the same regulations that apply to every member of the legal class and the judiciary, he is just one among others in the legal- and judicial sphere. Consequently, this can be seen as a limitation of the power of the ruler through law.[261]

Guy Burak focuses on the Ottoman period and demonstrates that the state played a central role in the lawmaking in that it assumed the authority to regulate and structure the official school, the *Ḥanafiyya*, which they adopted. In that endeavor the Ottomans intended to focus on a particular branch within the *ḥanafī* school of jurisprudence.[262] In order to regulate the legal content of that branch the Ottomans sought to create an imperial *madrasa* system with a specific curriculum that encompassed an imperial canon of texts. The result was the creation of an imperial learned hierarchy that was qualified to occupy judicial and bureaucratic positions, such as the position of the chief imperial *muftī* (*shaykh al-islām*). This state appointed chief *muftī* became the highest authority inside the imperial learned

---

[261] Fadel, "State and the Sharia," p. 99.
[262] Guy Burak, *The Second Formation of Islamic Law: The Hanafi School in the Early Modern Ottoman Empire* (New York: Cambridge University Press, 2015), p. 10.

hierarchy in both legal and scholarly matters, which allowed him to heavily regulate the

imperial canon, and thus, the doctrine of that particular *ḥanafī* branch. With the support of

a decree by the ruler, the chief *muftī* was even able to oblige the members of the judiciary

to adjudicate according to a minority opinion within the school.[263] According to Burak the

direct intervention of the state in the lawmaking process is not in the sense that the state

creates new content, but rather in the way that the state picks and chose from a variety of

norms found in the *ḥanafī* school.

Ibrahim showed that the intervention of the state in the lawmaking process was a

common practice under the Ottomans, as well as under the Mamluks. Both dynasties

selected between procedures or substantive laws to widen the scope of possible legal

outcomes or to guarantee certain legal outcomes. This was achieved through the

institutionalization of the four *madhāhib* (pl. of *madhhab*) in form of four chief judges and

"pragmatic eclecticism".

When the Ottomans conquered Egypt, they found an institutionalized pluralistic

legal system in the form of the Mamluk four chief *qāḍīs*, which was an interesting

mechanism to offer flexibility. After a more or less unsuccessful attempt of *"ḥanafization"*

in the Egyptian lands by the Ottomans to homogenize the law, they recognized the merits

of the flexible and pragmatic system. Ibrahim talks about what he calls "pragmatic

eclecticism", where the laity was permitted to select the forum of adjudication in court in

accordance with the doctrine *tatabbuʿ al-rukhaṣ* (school boundary-crossing), independent

of one's own school affiliation. This system allowed people to conduct legal transactions

that are not permitted by their own school of jurisprudence to be handled by a judge of

another *madhhab*, that permits such a legal transaction.[264] Ibrahim demonstrates that under

---

[263] Ibid., p. 11-12.
[264] Ibrahim, *Pragmatism in Islamic law*, p. 129-130. Pragmatic eclecticism was not only utilized by the elite, but also by

the Ottomans the *ḥanafī madhhab* assumed a "semi-default status", meaning that the huge majority of cases were handled by a *ḥanafī* judge, unless there was a motivation to reach a particular legal outcome that could only be achieved through another *madhhab*.[265]

Hoexter makes the case to show that *qāḍīs* and the ruler continued to play an important role in the evolution of Islamic law, even after what dominant historiography calls a constitutional agreement. Contrary to the common assumption that after that particular point in time the *qāḍī* and the ruler were deprived of that function and instead interpreting and evolving the law supposedly became the exclusive domain of the *fuqahā'* and the *muftīs*. Her article is based on traces left by the decisions of rulers and *qāḍīs* in the *fiqh*-literature.[266]

In that connection, the two topics of difference of opinion (*ikhtilāf*) and the role of custom (*'urf, 'āda*) in Islamic law are of central importance. The latter was not only regarded as a source of Islamic law, but also served as a fundamental vehicle and justification to accommodate social and economic change.[267] Rulers' decrees (*qānūn*) that were legitimated through the doctrine of *siyāsa*, were first and foremost seen as codification of customary law and custom is allowed under *fiqh*, as long as it does not contradict agreed upon principles of the Sharia.[268]

The accumulation of the *qāḍīs* rulings concerning similar cases could lead to the

---

the non-elite masses of the society (p. 156).

[265] Ibid., p. 149.

[266] Hoexter, *Qāḍī, Muftī* and Ruler: Their Roles in the Development of Islamic Law," p. 68-69. See also p. 80-82.

[267] Ibid., p. 70. See footnote number 10 for custom as a source of law. Look also at p. 71, for justifications for the reliance on custom provided by al-Sarakhsī (d. 1090 CE), Ibn Nujaim (d. 1561 CE) and al-Ḥaṣkafī (d. 1677 CE); See further Shabana, Ayman. *Custom in Islamic law and Legal Theory: The Development of the Concepts of 'Urf and 'Ādah in the Islamic Legal Tradition.* New York: Palgrave Macmillan, 2010, and Meshal, Reem A. *Sharia and the Making of the Modern Egyptian: Islamic Law and Custom in the Courts of Ottoman Cairo.* Cairo: The American University in Cairo Press, 2014.

[268] Uriel Heyd, *Studies in Old Ottoman Criminal Law,* (Oxford: Clarendon Press, 1973), p. 168; Shalakany, "Islamic Legal Histories," p. 73. The relevant legal maxims regarding the role of custom in Islamic law are "Custom is legal text", "Custom is one of the Sharia proofs in matters on which there is no written authority", and "What the believers consider right is right with God".

establishment of an informal "established/popular custom" (*ta'āmul, ta'āruf*). Afterwards, at a later stage, *muftīs* would discuss that custom and give it a "*shar'ī* framework" and thus, making it part of the Islamic substantive law (*furū'*).[269] The ruler on the other hand had the authority to end legal indeterminacy if there were several competing legal opinions regarding a legal issue. In cases of differences of opinions among the scholars, it was the rulers' prerogative to decide which opinion should be binding in courts.[270] Hoexter's findings provide a very interesting picture of a legal process that features the *qāḍī*, the religious scholars, such as *muftīs*, and the ruler. In fact, we could even include the common people and the laity in that process. The accumulation of judgments is the result of changing socio-economic factors that caused people to bring a specific issue to court so many times that the *qāḍīs* had to address it and find a proper solution for it, even if these solutions were not available in the *fiqh* discourse. According to Hoexter, in a later stage it was authors of *fatāwa* and *furū'* works who adopted the creative solutions of the *qāḍīs* and gave them a proper *shar'ī* framework through the tools and arguments of legal methodology (*uṣūl al-fiqh*), of which the source of custom and the notion of "changing times" was of fundamental importance. Through this process, change was incorporated into a legal school and the new opinion could be applied to similar cases in the future. Therefore, we could say that the common people and the *qāḍī* would stand in the beginning of a process of change. They would initiate that process and legal scholars, such as *muftīs* or other authors of *fiqh* works would stand in the middle of that process, and the ruler would be at the closing end, because he had the last word in the case of differences of

---

[269] Hoexter, "*Qāḍī, Muftī* and Ruler: Their Roles in the Development of Islamic Law," p. 72. Look at p. 72-74 for Hoexter's example on "cash-*waqfs*" and how Shaykh al-Islām Abū al-Su'ūd justified that new practice "on the grounds of it being a popular custom (*ta'āmul, ta'āruf*) and *istiḥsān*."

[270] Ibid., p. 78-79.

opinions.[271]

In a similar vein that Hoexter describes how *qāḍī* decisions and rulers' decrees found their way into *fiqh* works, we can describe the work of Samy Ayoub. He demonstrates how rulers' decrees were discussed by late *ḥanafī* jurists of the 17th and 18th centuries and thus incorporated into the *ḥanafī* legal discourse. He further argues that these decrees had a substantial impact on *ḥanafī* doctrines, especially in cases of juristic disputes and questions according to which legal opinion a judge should rule.[272] The Ottoman ruler had the "authority to limit a judge's ruling to a specific time, place, litigants, case, or to a specific opinion."[273]

Taking Ottoman Egyptian court practice in cases of child-custody as an example, Ibrahim shows that the judge had a certain degree of discretion, which he used in the sense of an "overriding principle" in order to assure the best interest of the child (*maṣlaḥat al-ṭifl*), even if it meant to depart or contradict the rules of jurists found in the *fiqh*-discourse.[274] This is a very intriguing example regarding the question of what constitutes Islamic normativity. As we have demonstrated in the previous chapter the dominant historiography of Islamic law only views theory in the form of the jurists' *fiqh*-discourse as Islamic normativity and everything that departs from that in practice is thus described as a deviation from normative discourse. However, Ibrahim argues here to treat Ottoman court practice as part of Islamic normativity, similar to legal precedent in the common-law tradition, instead of viewing Islamic law as a body of rules.[275] The principle of best interest of the child works like a practical *qawā'id fiqhiyya* in guiding the judge. An interesting

---

[271] Ibid., p. 84-85.
[272] Samy Ayoub, "The Sulṭān Says: State Authority in the Late Ḥanafī Tradition," *Islamic Law and Society* 23 (2016): p. 241.
[273] Ibid., p. 277.
[274] Ahmed Fekry Ibrahim, "The Best Interest of the Child in Pre-Modern Islamic Juristic Discourse and Practice," *The American Journal of Comparative Law* 63 (2016): p. 890.
[275] Ibid., p. 891.

question would be to further investigate whether or not the cases studied by Ibrahim found their way in the discussions of the *fiqh*-discourse and whether that caused a change in the discourse or not. Did that create new normativity in the *fiqh*-literature? What does this tell us about the structure of the law and the institutions of the law? Such questions lie outside the scope of this paper, but are worth pursuing in another thesis.

Guy Burak, Jackson and "pragmatic eclecticism" give the state the right to pick and choose from the doctrines created by jurists of the four schools, but he could not create his own norms. However, the state, the Ottoman state in particular, could intervene at times in the legal discourse and regulate some doctrinal matters. For example, settling disputes among jurists, which made him the final reference point. Jurists acknowledged the ruler as such, a legal authority, and they engaged his edicts in their literature.

Hoexter shows how the influence of custom norms that are not found in the works of the four schools of law could develop and find their way into the *fiqh*-discourse after some time. Which is a very intriguing example of how practice could influence doctrine and create legal change. That means that the judge had to have some kind of discretion, as is shown by Ibrahim in his article on child custody, where the decision of the judge does not follow the letter of the norms found in *fiqh*, but rather the principle of "best interests of the child".

Institutions of *siyāsa* and Criminal Law

The examples above show that we cannot speak about a dichotomy between Islamic law and jurists on one side, and political authority on the other side, as is argued by the dominant historiography. There was no division of labor in the sense that the ruler was not allowed to interfere in the jurists' endeavor of "creating" the law, and thereby deciding what the Sharia is. Instead, we have seen that the ruler played an active role in the lawmaking process, as a legal authority, by employing procedural or administrative measures, such as regulating and limiting the scope of judges, legal doctrine and the applicability of certain "opinions" found in the vast corpus of *fiqh*.

Qasim Zaman even argues that there was continuous participation of the ruler in legal matters and in the religious life even after the inquisition (*miḥna*). In his opinion, it is not possible to speak about a separation between religion and politics, as indicated by the dominant historiography.[276]

When talking about the relationship between the ruler and the religious scholars (*'ulamā'*), Hoexter talks about a *modus vivendi* that is similar to the quasi constitutional arrangement described by the dominant historiography. However, she emphasizes that this relationship was characterized by mutual dependence, respect and cooperation, where rulers for example sought advice from scholars on a number of issues. Rulers and scholars did not sever relations and they often pursued the same interests.[277]

It is not possible to identify jurists as the only stakeholders in the area of lawmaking, not even in *fiqh*, because as we have seen in Ayoub's example, the rulers' edicts had a fundamental impact in the discussions of jurists. Opposite to that, *siyāsa* is usually described as the domain of the state, but we will see that jurists had some influence here as well. Even though, jurists acknowledged that taxation, army organization etc. fall under the ruler's prerogative, this does not mean that jurists themselves had nothing to say about this.[278]

On the contrary, which leads us to our next discussion on criminal law in the light

---

[276] Muhammad Qasim Zaman, "The Caliphs, the 'Ulamā', and the Law: Defining the Role and Function of the Caliph in the Early 'Abbāsid Period," in *The Formation of Islamic Law*, ed. Wael B. Hallaq. (Aldershot: Ashgate/Variorum, 2004), p. 2-3; See also Lev, Yaacov. "Symbiotic Relations: Ulama and the Mamluk Sultans." *Mamluk Studies Review* XIII (2009): 1–26.

[277] Hoexter, "*Qāḍī, Muftī* and Ruler: Their Roles in the Development of Islamic Law," p. 78.

[278] "Professor Jonathan Brown: Is there Justice Outside God's Law? SOAS University London," YouTube Video, min. 34:56-35:20 and min. 35:38-35:45.

of *siyāsa* and its institutions, like the *muḥtasib*, different *siyāsa* courts, and alternative articulations on evidence and procedure. We will see that the boundaries between the sphere of the ruler and the sphere of jurists is not always clear cut and that we will come across overlapping spheres between the two.

For example, the substance and the guidelines for the *muḥtasib*, a "secular" institution according to the dominant historiography, come from the *fiqh*-discourse of jurists, in that he is expected to prevent things in public that go against *fiqh*-law.[279] Furthermore, Kristen Stilt's analyses of the *muḥtasib* of Mamluk Cairo sheds further light on the relationship between the religious scholars and the state. The *muḥtasib* was a shared institution and relied on both, manuals that came from the *fiqh* tradition and the ruler's policies and orders. In her work, she focuses on historical chronicles and legal sources, and presents us with several case studies that are related to the *muḥtasib`s* daily activities. Stilt demonstrates that rulers were not only involved in the religious culture, but also had religious concerns such as the proper conduct of ritual prayers or the regulation of sexual propriety in the public.[280] Another important aspect of her work is to show the influence of non-legal considerations and the importance of discretion on behalf of the *muḥtasib* in his daily actions. In that regard, the *muḥtasib* himself became a participant in the lawmaking process. Through his personal discretion, he decided on the spot what measure is appropriate to realize the aims of the Sharia. Even if the course of action he opts for in a specific situation is not to be found in the deliberations of *fiqh*, we cannot say that his actions are therefore "secular" in the sense of not being part of the Sharia. We could even regard his discretion as filling the gap in form of *ta`zīr* that was consciously left in the *fiqh*

---

[279] Ibid., min. 35:38-35:45.
[280] Kristen Stilt, *Islamic Law in Action: Authority, Discretion, and Everyday Experiences in Mamluk Egypt* (New York: Oxford University Press, 2012), p. 38-39.

literature.

Regarding another "secular" institution, the *maẓālim*-courts, Rapoport does not perceive a gap between the jurisdiction of the Sharia courts and the *maẓālim* or other courts that were established by the ruler. Instead, he claims that the system of the four chief judges under the Mamluks is a starting point of the integration of both systems. The introduction of this system by the ruler allowed for more flexibility, predictability and made the legal system more practical. Through the four-school system one could take advantage of the various elements of each school's legal doctrine.[281]

Concerning *maẓālim* courts Rapoport writes that *maẓālim* courts were created originally for the purpose of remedying administrative failures, but in the late Mamluk period they also dealt with commercial cases and cases of family law.[282] The purview of *maẓālim* courts incorporated the functions of the crimes courts as well. This is also Jalāl al-Dīn al-Dawānī's understanding. For him the *maẓālim* court is also the *jarāʾim* court and therefore, the *maẓālim* courts are connected to the *siyāsa* authority of the ruler.[283]

By the end of the Mamluk period the ruler's presence in the administration of justice grew stronger. Justice in the sense of justice of the Sharia and not justice according to the formal rules of *fiqh*. This trend continued to such an extent that rulers interpreted substantive rules of the Sharia without taking into consideration the opinions of the jurists.[284] When talking about the *siyāsa* courts and the *qāḍī* courts, Rapoport views the formers emphasis on equity and the latters emphasis on formalism as the main distinct feature between the two.[285] In Rapoport's narrative, the state and his *siyāsa sharʿiyya* is not

---

[281] Yossef Rapoport, "Royal Justice and Religious Law: *Siyāsah* and Shariʿah under the Mamluks," *Mamluk Studies Review* 16 (2012): p. 77-79.

[282] Ibid., p. 84.

[283] "Professor Jonathan Brown: Is there Justice Outside God's Law? SOAS University London," YouTube Video, min. 24:25-24:47.

[284] Rapoport, "Royal Justice and Religious Law," p. 97.

[285] Ibid., p. 75.

an "external intrusion" into the lawmaking process which is believed to have been a privilege of the jurists, but rather, the state plays an active role in "adapting ..., the shari'ah, to social practice."[286]

Fadel argues that therefore it is more fitting to assume that the conflict between ruler and jurists was not a conflict where the secular clashed with the religious, but instead we can talk about two competing visions and conceptions of Islamic authority and Islamic justice.[287]

Brown refers to crimes courts that were talked about by legal scholars in their writings, called *wilayat al-jarā'im* by Māwardī (d. 1058 CE) and others, which become institutionalized around the 800 CE during the Abbasid era.[288] These courts only dealt with the most serious crimes, such as those mentioned in Koran chapter 5, verse 33 that include *hirāba* (banditry, highway robbery) or first degree premeditated murder (*ghīla*) according to the *mālikī* school of law. The same verse even mentions several severe punishments for perpetrators who fall under its purview, like the death penalty, crucifixion, and the cutting of hands and feet in opposite directions.[289]

This verse is believed to be revealed in the context of a *hadīth* (the *hadīth* of 'Uraniyīn). According to that report people came to the Prophet in Medina and the climate was unpleasant for them, so the Prophet send them to rest and refresh themselves next to some camels.[290] The report continues as follows:[291]

"...They then fell upon the shepherds and killed them and turned apostates from Islam

---

[286] Ibid.

[287] Fadel, "State and the Sharia," p. 100.

[288] "Professor Jonathan Brown: Is there Justice Outside God's Law? SOAS University London," YouTube Video, min. 13:41-14:12; Rohe, *Islamic Law in Past and Present*, p. 52.

[289] Ibid., min. 14:48-16:10.

[290] Ibid., min. 16:13-16:45.

[291] Abdullah Saeed, "Pre-modern Islamic Legal Restrictions on Freedom of Religion, with Particular Reference to Apostasy and its Punishment, "In *Islamic Law and International Human Rights Law*, ed. Anver M. Emon et al. (Oxford: Oxford University Press, 2013), p. 237.

and drove off the camels of the Prophet. This news reached the Prophet and he sent [people] on their track, and they were [brought] and handed over to him. He [the Prophet] required their hands and their feet be cut off, and put out their eyes, and they were left on the stony ground to die."[292]

As we see, the perpetrators received the punishment for waging war against God and the Prophet that is mentioned in Koran 5:33.

This Koranic verse and the prophetic example constitute the basis for the criminal courts. What is also important to notice here is that there is no limit to the punishment, even up to execution. This specific incident is cited as an expression of *siyāsa* by the Prophet himself, pointed towards by jurists. According to judges the Prophet here dealt with a crime that is unique and requires unique punishment. Those kinds of cases do not fall under the scope of the *qāḍī*, but rather under the scope of the ruler, who in contrast to the *qāḍī* possesses the means to deal with them.[293]

Ibn Taymiyya speaks about the same kind of issue. In his time those crimes courts were called "war/military courts". In his description of them he says that those courts deal with very problematic cases that would usually fall under the *qāḍī*'s jurisdiction, but he does not have the means or sufficient evidence to solve them.[294]

According to Brown, the difference between the two, the "*siyāsa*" courts and the *qāḍī*-court lie in the restrictions put on the judge. Whereas the judge in the *qāḍī*-court is bound by his respective school of law, the judges of the *maẓālim/jarā'im* court are not. Those restrictions had the functions of check and balances on the judge, in order to prevent arbitrary and unfair rulings. One of those limitations on the *qāḍī* in the Sharia court was for

---

[292] Ibid., p. 237.
[293] "Professor Jonathan Brown: Is there Justice Outside God's Law? SOAS University London," YouTube Video, min. 16:55-18:27.
[294] Ibid., min. 18:28-19:04.

example that the he was not allowed to base his judgment on his own knowledge.[295]

So, on the one side those restrictions protect the innocent from unsubstantiated accusations from the judge, but at the same time this severely cumbers the judge's ability to convict a guilty person.[296]

Under *fiqh* two upstanding male witnesses are required, in order to convict a person for murder. If we look at who is permitted as a witness in murder trials under *fiqh*, we will see that this leads to very serious issues in the persecution of murder. If for example the only witnesses of a murder are women or children, then it is impossible to have a case.[297] As we have seen in the jurists' *fiqh*-discourse on evidence and proof, there is a huge emphasis on the "spoken word", which is manifest in the kinds of proofs that were seen as "the basis of a valid judgment", such as the defendant's confession, eye-witness testimony and the taking of oaths or the refusal to take an oath. External factors were included in order to determine the credibility of the "speaker" and his "words".[298] We have also seen that jurists allowed, although with clear limits, circumstantial evidence under *fiqh*.[299] Nevertheless, this *fiqh* based conception with its formalistic procedure and high evidentiary barriers for murder embodied a substantial challenge for the ruler to maintain law and order.[300]

In the following paragraphs, we will look at a shift that occurred in the discourse on evidence and procedure in the realm of Islamic normativity between the thirteenth and fourteenth centuries in Mamluk Egypt. Of particular importance in that regard was the

---

[295] Ibid., min 24:48-25:41. Johansen, "Signs as Evidence," p. 175-176. Whereas *hanafī* and *shāfi'ī* jurists generally accept the knowledge of the *qāḍī* as a type of proof, except in cases that fall under the category of *ḥuqūq Allāh*, jurists of the *mālikī* and *hanbalī* school of law do not regard the knowledge of the judge as proof.

[296] "Professor Jonathan Brown: Is there Justice Outside God's Law? SOAS University London," YouTube Video, min. 26:34-26:58.

[297] Ibid., min. 19:11-19:22.

[298] Johansen, "Signs as Evidence," p. 169. Although jurists reserved an epistemological skepticism towards the spoken word as indisputable certain truth.

[299] Ibid., p. 173-175.

[300] Shalakany, "Islamic Legal Histories," p. 69.

work of famous *mālikī* and *ḥanbalī* scholars, including al-Qarāfī, Ibn Taymiyya and Ibn Qayyim al-Jawziyya, and the doctrine of *siyāsa al-shar ʿiyya*. The reader should also be reminded of the tripartition of crimes in Criminal law under *fiqh* into *qiṣāṣ, ḥudūd,* and *ta ʿzīr*. Particularly the third one, *ta ʿzīr*, is important for our discussion, because it allowed for a vast amount of discretion regarding evidence and procedure.

According to the understanding of this "new doctrine" jurists have no monopoly in legal matters and moreover, the *fiqh*-corpus is not to be seen as the only manifestation of Islamic normativity.[301] The law expounded by jurists and expressed in the *fiqh* discourse is not by default the equivalent of "revealed normativity", unless it corresponds to indisputable scriptural texts. Otherwise, their opinions fall into the category of "free interpretation" and are only binding on their authors. Overall, the work of jurists "adds a dimension to revealed normativity but is neither its only nor its most important representation."[302]

Rather, every member of the state apparatus was obliged to dispense justice, and their considerations and interests constitute a legitimate basis for judgments in the same way as the norms of *fiqh* do. In particular, this means that the *fiqh*-based conception of proof and evidence, in which the judge depends on the "spoken word" of litigants and witnesses, is not seen as the only valid and possible Islamic normative conception of proof and evidence. Instead, those "new" scholars center their conception of such around circumstantial evidence in form of signs and indicators as sufficient proof and basis for judgment. Their main concern is to safeguard public interest and to enhance the state's ability to maintain law and order.[303] Political authorities are assigned a religious dimension

---

[301] Johansen, "Signs as Evidence," p.180.
[302] Ibid., p. 183.
[303] Ibid., p. 180.

and their strength is understood as a fundamental necessity for the ongoing existence and

religious practice of the community. In that sense, the duties of all public functions are

subsumed under the fulfillment of the *hisba*, meaning commanding the good and

forbidding the evil.[304]

Brown comes to the conclusion that according to al-Dawānī the Sharia includes not

only what is found in legal treatises in form of *fiqh* books, but also the laws and procedures

of *hisba*, *jarā'im* and *mazālim* courts, taxation, army etc. Because without all of that it is

not possible to guarantee the basic rights of people, such as their right to property, as the

people of Mosul.[305] Among the examples mentioned by al-Dawānī, who functioned as a

judge in the *mazālim* courts in Shiraz, in his treatise include cases of murder without any

witnesses. In order to solve those crimes, they interrogated suspects until they confessed.

Such interrogation was not possible in the *qāḍī* courts.[306]

Shalakany observes that there was "no religious rationale" dictating the division of

labor between jurists, *qāḍīs*, who rely on their norms derived from *fiqh*, and the state and

his agents who preserved law and order through additional means.[307] Nothing in the law

indicates a necessary separation of powers in the legal sphere between jurists and non-

jurists, rather every person "in a position of authority – including rulers, governors, and

market inspectors – participate in the implementation of Islamic law."[308] This includes the

admission of signs (*'alāmāt*) and indicators (*amārāt*) as legitimate proof in the religious

normative sense. Even further, the office of the *muhtasib* and courts legislated under the

siyāsa al-shar'iyya doctrine, as for example *mazālim* courts, are legitimate "Islamic" legal

---

[304] Shalakany, "Islamic Legal Histories," p. 70; Johansen, "Signs as Evidence," p. 181.
[305] "Professor Jonathan Brown: Is there Justice Outside God's Law? SOAS University London," YouTube Video, min. 39:04-39:37.
[306] Ibid., min. 39:40-40:12.
[307] Shalakany, "Islamic Legal Histories," p. 70.
[308] Rapoport, "Royal Justice and Religious Law," p. 93.

institutions.[309] By viewing the practice of the ruler, members of the military, and the

political and administrative elite as a potentially legitimate "interpretation of the revealed

normativity"[310], their notion of justice became an equally legitimate expression of Islamic

law as the notion of jurists. Furthermore, "Equating shari'ah with *fiqh*, and opposing them

to a political or secular *siyāsah*, creates the misperception that rulers did not have religious

concerns or influence, and that the jurists did not engage in considerations of public

welfare."[311]

The Spirit and the Letter of the Law

There was always potential tension between the ruler's discretion and some jurists'

conception of Sharia. This tension stems partly from an understanding of the Sharia as "a

body of law derivable by jurists strictly through disciplined scriptural hermeneutics,"[312]

coupled with a very narrow conception of *siyāsa*, in which the state is only designated to

pick and choose from the doctrines of the four schools of *fiqh*.

If however, one would view the Sharia in more general terms that is not only

restricted to the discourse of jurists, which is often characterized by a commitment to the

articulated rules of *fiqh* and formalism in the law, it would be possible to subsume notions

of equity and means to promote justice that are not explicit in texts, in an alternative

articulation of Sharia. The following incident dealing with the issue of debt should serve as

an example where different articulations of Sharia are applied and at the same time it will

---

[309] Shalakany, "Islamic Legal Histories," p. 70-71; Johansen, "Signs as Evidence," p. 188-189. See for more detail Johansen, p. 190-193.

[310] Johansen, "Signs as Evidence," p. 183.

[311] Rapoport, "Royal Justice and Religious Law," p. 75; Stilt, *Islamic Law in Action*, p. 26; Vogel, *Islamic Law and Legal System*, p. 171-172; Rapoport talks about an incident where a Jewish merchant complains to the sultan about a Mālikī judge who treated him unjustly. The judge, summoned by the sultan, defends himself by arguing that he only followed the Sharia in what he did, to which the sultan responded that the *siyāsa* "runs the same course as the shari'ah." In Rapoport, "Royal Justice and Religious Law," p. 87; Furthermore, there are several other examples of *siyāsa* officials, like chamberlains and military executives that show their concern for Islamic law. See Rapoport, "Royal Justice and Religious Law," p. 88-89.

[312] Anjum, "Siyasa al-Shar'iyya."

show us the limits of the jurists' formalism in the flexible four chief *qāḍī* system.

In the second half of the fourteenth century and in the fifteenth century, non- *qāḍī* court officials, such as military officers, and *siyāsa* courts experienced an expansion of their jurisdiction, through which they assumed a jurisdiction as wide as the jurisdiction of the *qāḍī* courts, including cases revolving around family law and debts.[313] The incident is reported by the chronicler al-Maqrīzī, who tells us that Persian merchants sold goods in Cairo and that the local merchants who bought from them, resold the goods without having paid the Persian merchants. The case is brought to court, presided by a *hanafī* judge, where the local merchants claimed that they were bankrupt. As a result, they were imprisoned until they were declared bankrupt or until the foreign merchants would leave Cairo. Either way, even the strictest of the four Sunni schools in regards to payment of debts, the *hanafī* school of law, allowed the debtors to get away without having to pay, which can be seen as the limits of *fiqh* at that time in dealing with debtors. The Persian merchants complained to the sultan, who assigned one of his agents, in this case the chamberlain (*hājib*), to deal with the issue. By presumably torturing the debtors, the chamberlain found out that they were hiding money, and thus the Persian merchants were able to receive their debts. This case shows what could be regarded as a "loophole" to escape payment, which was only possible due to the formalism of the *qāḍī* courts. At the end it was only due to *siyāsa* that an injustice "done" by a *qāḍī* was remedied.[314]

Some jurists in the Mamluk period objected to what they perceived as an infringement on the Sharia, while others endorsed the changes as "integral elements in the application of Islamic law."[315] Tāj al-Dīn al Subkī, for example criticized the practice of

---

[313] Rapoport, "Royal Justice and Religious Law," p. 75-76.
[314] Ibid., p.83-84.
[315] Ibid., p. 77.

police chiefs (*wālī*) of forcing a person who deflowers and impregnates a woman, to marry

her, justifying this on grounds of the future benefit of the unborn child. Subkī sees this

decision as going against the Sharia, according to which a child born out of fornication is

not to be recognized as the child of the fornicator. The correct ruling in Subkī's view

would have been a fine, "equal to the expected decrease in the bride's marriage gift

(*mahr*)."[316] Rapoport considers the solution offered by the police chiefs as a more just

solution in comparison to that offered by al-Subkī.[317] Nevertheless, it is evident that for al-

Subkī only jurists of the four schools of jurisprudence can deduce what the Sharia is and he

urges the ruler and his agents to only pick and choose from the doctrines of the four

schools of *fiqh* and not to go beyond those doctrines, lest they would overstep the

boundaries of the Sharia.[318]

As depicted in the child custody case mentioned above, the contradiction between

juristic discourse and practice is not only restricted to cases where *siyāsa* is involved, but

can also occur in *qāḍī* courts, where the judge is supposed to be bound by the doctrines of

fiqh. The case in question involves a woman, her husband and her ex-husband, who agreed

that the woman and her then-husband, who is a non-relative of the child, would have

custody over her daughter from her previous marriage. In exchange the ex-husband would

not have to provide child support. Discourse says that a woman would lose her right to

custody in case of remarriage to a non-relative of the child. From all the four schools of

jurisprudence only some jurists from the *mālikī* school accepted the possibility for a

woman to retain custody of her child, even in the case of remarriage, provided that the

father did not request custody within a year.[319]

---

[316] Ibid., p. 89.
[317] Ibid.
[318] Ibid., p. 94.
[319] Ibrahim, "The Best Interest of the Child in Pre-Modern Islamic Juristic Discourse and Practice," p. 886-887.

However, the agreement in this particular case went further than just granting the woman and the stepfather custody, but in addition it stipulated that the daughter would remain with the mother "regardless of whether or not she left the habitual residence of the child (that is, Cairo), and regardless of whether or not the father stayed in Cairo."[320]

According to the agreement the father would not have any possibility to take the daughter away from the mother, not even in the case of him moving away from Cairo. Along with custody, the mother also shared guardianship with the father over the common daughter, however, in contradiction to juristic discourse, which would allow the father to for example marry off his daughter, the mother had the last word in every decision regarding their daughter. The mother's presence and consent was required for every decision regarding the daughter. Even though, this agreement "clearly contradicted Sunni juristic discourse,"[321] the *mālikī* judge in the *qāḍī* court notarized the agreement.[322]

Authors of *fiqh* works assumed that a stepfather would have a hostile attitude towards a child who is unrelated to him. Because of that, author-jurists saw the best interests of the child by denying a remarrying mother to keep custody. Also, juristic discourse always privileged the father with having unrestricted guardianship in regards to all matters of the child.[323] Therefore, if the judge had followed the juristic discourse, meaning the letter of *fiqh*-rules, he could not have accepted and notarized the agreement. The judge however, did not choose to follow the formalism of *fiqh*, but instead followed the spirit of the law, because he regarded the private agreement as offering a "non-adversarial" solution and as being "inherently in the best interests of their children."[324]

---

[320] Ibid., p. 887.
[321] Ibid., p. 888.
[322] Ibid., p. 887-888.
[323] Ibid., p. 888.
[324] Ibid., p. 890.

Notions of Injustice

So far we talked about examples where deviating from and even contradicting juristic discourse provided a more "just" result than *fiqh*. But, what is with instances where the opposite is the case, meaning "unjust" practices of the rulers, as for example fratricide in the Ottoman empire or direct interventions by Mamluk sultans in cases of criminal law, such as the *ḥadd* punishment for adultery.

Throughout its history the Ottoman empire experienced several periods of interregnum with different members of the dynasty fighting each other over the throne, which resulted in the death of many people and endangered the very existence of the Empire. Sultan Mehmet the Conqueror (d. 1481 CE) instituted the practice of fratricide which allowed a ruler to kill those of his male relatives including brothers, who are most likely to challenge his legitimacy and bring about a war. This practice was justified with recourse to *maṣlaḥa mursala* [325] and the following edict from Sultan Mehmet:

> "And to whomsoever of my sons the Sultanate shall pass, it is fitting that for the order of the world he shall kill his brothers. Most of the Ulema allow it. So let them act on this."[326]

In 1513 CE an adultery case brought about a clash between sultan Qānṣūh and jurists about the appropriate punishment. Because the circumstances of the offense at hand

---

[325] Ekrem Buğra Ekinci, *Islam Hukuku* (Istanbul: Arı Sanat Yayınevi, 2006), p. 116-117; Donald Quataert, *The Ottoman Empire, 1700-1922* (Cambridge: Cambridge University Press, 2005), p. 91-92.

In favor of the practice some referred to the story of Moses and his unknown companion in Koran chapter 18, verses 80-81. Here, the companion of Moses kills an innocent child, whereupon Moses asks him how he could kill an innocent person who did not kill somebody else. Then the companion replies: "As for the lad, his parents were believers; and we were afraid he would impose on them insolence and unbelief; so we desired that their Lord should give to them in exchange one better than he in purity, and nearer in tenderness." Verses quoted from the translation of A. J. Arberry's *"The Koran interpreted"*.

In addition, those who invoke *maṣlaḥa* as a legitimate concern to kill innocent people, refer to the discussions about the killing of Muslim prisoners who are used as a shield by the enemy. Unless the Muslim army attacks, accepting the possibility of killing innocent Muslims, they would be defeated, which would lead to the invasion of the Muslim land, and as a result not only the Muslim prisoners, but all Muslims could be killed.

[326] Quataert, *The Ottoman Empire, 1700-1922*, p. 91, citing A. D. Alderson, The Structure of the Ottoman Dynasty (London, 1956), p. 25.

could not satisfy the high evidentiary demands for the *hadd* punishment for *zinā*, the case

was presumably tried under *ta'zīr* and accordingly it was ruled that "the two adulterers

should be beaten severely, fined, and led through the city on donkeys, facing

backwards."[327]

Sultan Qānṣūh however, regarded this verdict as too lenient and insisted that the

adulterers have to be punished according to the prescribed punishment for *zinā* as is stated

in Islamic law, meaning stoning to death. The jurists opposed the sultan on this matter by

referring to the established rules of evidence and procedure for *hudūd* offenses, which were

not met in the case at hand. Nonetheless, the sultan dismissed the jurists' arguments and

ordered the execution of the adulterers.[328]

We are not attempting to idealize the practice of the ruler and his officials as a

better form of justice than that of the jurists. Rather, we want to argue to consider both

forms of justice as equally legitimate expressions and attempts to implement Islamic law,

without favoring one over the other. It goes without saying that not every ruling or practice

is by default an acceptable expression of Islamic law, which is implicated in the separation

between *siyāsa 'ādila* and *siyāsa ẓālima*. So, in principle *siyāsa*, just as *fiqh* is a legitimate

way to articulate the Sharia. In contrast to *fiqh* however, there is no systematic and broadly

acknowledged theory in order to distinguish which results are acceptable and which are

not.

Not every *ijtihād* in *fiqh* is allowed to act upon and those opinions are classified as

deviant (*shādh*). With *siyasa* however, the borders between what is legitimate and what is

illegitimate is not clear cut. Even the distinction between *siyāsa 'ādila* and *siyāsa ẓālima* is

not sufficient, because some scholars have a very narrow understanding of what falls

---

[327] Rapoport, "Royal Justice and Religious Law," p. 100.
[328] Ibid.

within the category of *siyāsa 'ādila*, such as those for example who deem *siyasa* only acceptable as long as it is restricted to the picking and choosing from the vast corpus of *fiqh*-opinions, or filling the gaps left by *fiqh*.

However, it is beyond the scope of this paper to assess which particular action or decision is the most correct and best expression of Islamic law. Since we regard Islamic law as a legal system that changes throughout time and place, and because Islamic law is the result of several actors involved in the lawmaking process, a past ruling could have been perceived as a correct expression of Islamic law, but viewed by some contemporary or later generations of Muslims as a wrong expression of Islamic law.[329]

Whereas on the one hand it is possible to back the sultan's fratricide by invoking *maṣlaḥa mursala*, arguing that rebellion and war is worse than the killing of one or a few, on the other hand one could counter this by saying that it is not acceptable to kill a person for a crime he or she did not commit, and that the mere concern about a potential uprising in the future cannot justify the killing of an innocent person, particularly a child.

For people belonging to those generations who experienced infightings of the dynasty that almost brought the empire to the brink of collapse, it might have been a legitimate concern to accept this cruel practice of fratricide, despite of the bloodshed of "innocent" people and the potential for legal abuse.[330]

With changing circumstances and new generations who did not go through the same experience this perception might have changed, and they considered the damage of that practice as too disproportionate and sought a more suitable alternative. The damage that is talked about here is not restricted to the cruelty of this practice, but also to further

---

[329] Such as Asad writes: "Argument and conflict over the form and significance of practices are therefore a natural part of any Islamic tradition." See p. 22 in his essay "The Idea of an Anthropology of Islam."

[330] For an opinion that argues why fratricide could not be envisioned by *maṣlaḥa mursala*, see Mehmet Akman, *Osmanli Devletinde Kardeş Katli*. Istanbul: Eren, 1997, p. 155-156.

concerns, such as the potential lack of adult successors to the throne in the case of death of the ruling sultan.

As a result, with one exception, the practice of fratricide in the Ottoman empire effectively ended in 1648 and was replaced with the "gilded cage" (*kafes*), meaning that when the eldest male became sultan, the other males were kept alive, but their freedom to move was restricted to the palace.[331]

What is the yardstick then in order to assess which kind of action in Islamic law can count as Islamic and which not? This is not what this paper is claiming to answer. But, we question the notion that only what is sanctioned by jurists could be Islamic law. The action taken in the case of child custody presented by Ibrahim and the way the chamberlain dealt with the debtors in Mamluk Egypt present examples where justice was achieved by ways not envisaged in the norms of the four schools of jurisprudence. Here, the formalism of *fiqh* obstructed the very purpose of the Sharia.

On the other hand, Sultan Qānṣūh's harsh stance in the case of *zinā* shows the potential of arbitrary judgments and legal abuse, that can occur if the formalism of *fiqh* is totally ignored. This particular example along with the others we looked, also reveal the political dimension involved with the question regarding legal authority, which is pointed out by Vogel:

> "A vital issue (both Islamically and otherwise) is to ask how the scholars' representations, their doctrines, are a function of their efforts to consolidate fiqh's control over power, or—what is from their perspective the same thing—to advance their own authority over other social forces. For all these reasons sound method demands that we approach an Islamic legal system from more than one angle, separately according to the differing perspectives

---

[331] Quataert, The Ottoman Empire, 1700-1922, p. 91-92.

of its various actors. "[332]

Therefore, we should not be satisfied with a very narrow notion of Islamic normativity, that is only the discourse of jurists. Rather, we should incorporate the notions of other actors as well, with the caveat that there might be some "unjust" practices and rulings and that not everything a Muslim ruler does for example is by default an expression of the Sharia. Those non-jurists discourses and notions of the Sharia however, should be regarded as legitimate in so far, as they are one among several other discourses inside the broader discourse of Islamic law, which is an ongoing process characterized by the interaction and relationship of those diverse actors over the correct expression of Islamic law.

This more abstract conception of Sharia that is not confined to the letter of specific texts found in scripture, allows for a broader definition of Islamic legitimacy, which goes beyond the norms of the four schools of jurisprudence. In that regard it is also not a requirement to base one's decision on an individual norm found in legal manuals of *fiqh*, instead, the point of reference for such a decision could be "broad general principles" that are in line with and promote the aims of the Sharia (*maqāsid al-sharī'a*). Moreover, this vision of Sharia does not limit the dispensation of justice in the name of the "revealed law" to the judge (*qāḍī*) who presides in the *qāḍī*-courts and depends on the *fiqh* of the four schools of jurisprudence. Scholars such as Ibn Taymiyya and Shihāb al-Dīn al-Qarāfī for example subsumed every major administrative and political official that had the authority to issue decisions and impose sanctions or obligations under the term judge (*ḥākim* or *qāḍī*). Because at the end, all officials who acted as "judges" were seen in their function to command what is good and to forbid what is evil, whether it is the *qāḍī* in the *qāḍī* -courts,

---

[332] Frank E. Vogel, *Islamic Law and Legal System: Studies of Saudi Arabia* (Leiden: Brill, 2000), p. 171.

the market inspector, the vizier, tax collectors, high ranking army officer, or the head of state himself.[333] The following quote from the *ḥanbalī* scholar Ibn ʿAqīl (d. 1119 CE) that stems from a discussion he had with a *shāfiʿī* scholar regarding the relationship between governance and the revealed law, demonstrates the broad conceptions of Sharia in a very nice manner:

> "Government is that activity whereby people are enabled to tend toward good and away from evil, even if the Apostle had not instituted it, or if it had not been the object of a revealed law. Now if by your statement "except that which agrees with the revealed law," you mean an administration that does not contradict the revealed law, then that would be right; but if you mean that there is no valid administration except that which is stated explicitly in the revealed law, that would be wrong."[334]

Now we will return to the definition of Sharia. In its broadest sense, Sharia entails the totality of the Islamic religion, including theology, spirituality, but also commands and prohibitions by God in his scripture. In most cases, however, those injunctions and norms lack detail and are not very explicit, but rather ambiguous. Because of that it is more fitting to talk about legal indicants that point towards the law in the mind of God.

In a second, very restricted sense, we can talk about Sharia as a synonym of *fiqh*. Here, in theory, God is the legislator of the law, but in practice, it is jurists of the schools of jurisprudence deriving the law from divine scriptural sources, through the application of a certain legal theory. A legal theory, that deals with and expands on the legal indicants mentioned above, in order to come up with a law that has a divine basis. In this case, it is more accurate to speak about *fiqh*, which compared to Sharia is not fallible and is a human

---

[333] Baber Johansen, "A Perfect Law in an Imperfect Society: Ibn Taymiyya's Concept of "Governance in the Name of the Sacred Law"," in *The Law Applied: Contextualizing the Islamic Shari'a: A Volume in Honor of Frank E. Vogel*, ed. Frank E. Vogel et al. (Leiden: I.B. Tauris, 2008), p. 268-269.

[334] Ibid., p. 269; Ibn Qayyim, *al-Ṭuruq al-Ḥukmiyya fī al-Siyāsa al-Sharʿiyya*, p. 29.

process. If we were to adopt this understanding of the Sharia as the sole legitimate articulation of Islamic law, then we could in fact say that Islamic law is a jurists' law. However, this endeavor of *fiqh*, does not deal with every imaginable area of life, theology, spirituality, and even law, because scripture does not offer legal indicants regarding every topic. Which means that according to this understanding, there cannot be an Islamic law on some questions, such as in regards to a number of very important administrative or constitutional questions. As such, "the Sharia", would not allow for a practical way of governance that could effectively respond to social change. This understanding of Sharia is central to the dominant historiography and its two premises as described by Shalakany and that we attempted to challenge.

In the light of our discussion, which aside from legal discourses of jurists, touched upon legal practice, the role of the state, non-jurists, discretion, and non-strictly legal factors, we can argue for a broader understanding of Sharia. An understanding that goes beyond the second understanding (Sharia as synonymous to *fiqh*) and includes *siyāsa*, the actions of the state and his agents, and the instances of discretion of said actors. Such an understanding represents a better reflection of "the law" that was "actually" applied in premodern Muslim societies.

Conclusion

The state and its representatives in the legal sphere, such as judges or *muḥtasibs*, tried to accommodate the needs of society as much as they could and opted to make peoples' lives easier, instead of creating hardship, as long as the integrity of indisputable tenets of the Sharia, in form of unequivocal texts (*nuṣūṣ*, pl. of *naṣṣ*) was preserved. This could not be done with a body of fixed rules, but rather with a legal system that operates according to certain principles. This was justified through a broader understanding of what constitutes a legitimate legal basis in Islam. Whereas some scholars and even rulers like Nūr al-Dīn Zankī, were convinced that only what is explicit in scripture provides a legitimate basis, other scholars, such as Ibn Taymiyya, argued for a broader conception of Islamic legitimacy. According to the latter, even benefits or interests that are not mentioned in explicit texts of scripture can serve as a legitimate basis, as long as they do not violate unequivocal texts and serve towards the fulfillment of the aims of the Sharia.

What does that mean regarding the questions who is regarded to be among the legal actors in the lawmaking process, what constitute sources for lawmaking, and what are sources for the study of the history of Islamic law? As such, legal actors are not only madrasa educated jurists, but also the head of state, judges of *siyāsa* courts, *muhtasibs* and even the laity. We are left with several equally valid interpretations of Islamic law. In that regard, legal sources are not restricted to the writings of jurists, such as legal manuals. Instead, we can count court judgments in general, decisions of the ruler and his agents among legal sources as well. Concerning the study of the history of Islamic law, this entails that we should not confine ourselves to works of *fiqh* alone, but expand the array of sources to be studied including among others court records, collections of rulers' decisions, and every kind of imaginable records from which one could hope to filter information on the application of the law, as done by Stilt, who relied heavily on chronicles.

CHAPTER FOUR

Conclusion

Dominant Historiography

The dominant historiography conceptualizes Islamic law as the law of jurists. Their understanding narrows down the kind of sources we can use in order to study the history of

Islamic Law. Accordingly, only what was produced by jurists could tell us about Islamic law, its contents, and its legitimate sources. As a consequence, the state, the society and non-jurists are disregarded as actors in shaping Islamic law. In addition to viewing Islamic law as the primary domain of jurists, this understanding describes Islamic Law as a sacred law, meaning that religious texts constitute the sole bases for law-making in Islam. Thus, everything that is not mentioned in scripture or cannot be traced back to it, does not count as Islamic law. What constitutes a scriptural basis is decided by an ideal legal theory created by jurists, *uṣūl al-fiqh*, whose primary sources are the Koran and the prophetic Sunna. According to that legal theory, *qiyās* is the only means to extend the rationale of scripture to new questions. At some point in history, Islamic law supposedly reached a point where every possible question was solved and the gate of *ijtihād* (independent reasoning) became closed, which prevented change in Islamic law and made it impossible to find practical solutions to an ever-changing environment. This caused the ruling authorities to come up with their own parallel legal system that was more practical for governance, which lead to a growing gap between legal theory and legal practice in Islamic lands. In summary, we can say, this dominant historiography bears a lot of underlying assumptions and premises: Islamic law is a "scriptural" law, only jurists play a role in deciding what Islamic law is, consequently the legal treatises of jurists tell us what Islamic law is. Further, Islamic law is a sacred law that defies change, especially after the closure of the gate of *ijtihād*. The state does not partake in the formation of Islamic law and the state's law-making authority, called *siyāsa*, is secular as opposed to the sacred Islamic law. Therefore, in order to know what Islamic law is and to study its history, we have to look at the theoretical legal discourse in form of works authored by jurists, such as legal manuals, rather than looking at legal practice or the role of the state.

Non-Orientalist Group One

However, a number of notions of the dominant historiography was challenged by subsequent scholarship. Particularly regarding their assumptions on legal change in Islamic law. Scholars have shown that in the confines of *fiqh* legal change was always possible, even after the supposed closure of the gate of *ijtihād*. The mechanisms to achieve legal change became different under the regime of *taqlīd*. *Taqlīd* should therefore be understood as making Islamic law more predictable, which shows that Islamic law became a mature legal system. As such, one characteristic is that law does not change easily in order to guarantee a high degree of predictability.

Even though, this stream of scholarship challenges several views of the dominant group, they nevertheless, confine themselves to the framework of the same group that they are criticizing. This is true in so far as they do not challenge their premises strong enough, which becomes evident when we look at the answers of both groups regarding the question of legal actors of Islamic law, its legitimate sources and its sources to study the history of Islamic law. In conclusion, this is a narrative that focuses on jurists as the legitimate interpreters of the Sharia and excludes the state and his agents in that process.

Non Orientalist Group Two

This group is free of dichotomies such as "religious vs. secular". By emphasizing the role of the state and the integration of legal practice they widen our field of actors in the lawmaking process, which at the same time widens the legitimate sources for lawmaking, including among others the secondary sources of *uṣūl al-fiqh*, *siyāsa* and custom. At the same time this expands the scope of literature and sources for the study of the history of Islamic law, such as court records.

If we want to have a direct reflection of legal practice, in the sense of law as applied in courts, or law dispensed by any kind of state authority, then we have to look into different sources, such as *qāḍīs'* judgments that were registered in local courts, the collections of rulers' decrees, and even chronicles that can include some very intriguing information on the actions of the *muḥtasib* and more. With regards to legal practice, even works authored by jurists, such as works of substantive law (*furū'*) or *fatāwā* collections that present us a picture of the theoretical discourse, show traces of, and were probably inspired by real incidents, because as we have seen in the Ottoman period, the rulers' decrees in form of *qānūn* or *qāḍīs'* judgments found their ways into their discourses.

By revisiting the question of who participates in the lawmaking and by widening the sources of Islamic law beyond the scriptural texts, one can no longer argue that Islamic law is a pure sacred or religious law. Parts of it, like rituals, are certainly religious, but Islamic law also covers a broad range of areas that we find in the non-religious law of nation-states. This area of Islamic law could therefore be called "secular", in the sense that areas, such as trade, army organization or criminal investigation do not primarily revolve around the relationship between a believer and God.

The purpose of the thesis was not to propose a new theory in order to explain what Islamic law is, but rather to argue for a broader understanding of Sharia as being more than just the *fiqh* of jurists. In this thesis, we have attempted to show this by looking at examples of legal practice, the role of the state, and theoretical discourses of jurists.

Generally, Islamic legal history had its main interest in the works of jurists, but also in certain periods, particularly the "formative period" and the legal reforms of the nineteenth century.[335]

We tried to look at that relatively understudied period that lies between the two and

---

[335] Burak, *The Second Formation of Islamic Law*, p. 220.

saw a more complex picture of Islamic law, one that challenges the notions of Islamic law being frozen in time, that Islamic law was irrelevant for the legal systems in Muslim lands, that Islamic legal theory reached its final form with al-Shāfiʿī, that Islamic law was unpractical, rigid and too ideal for criminal law etc.

Instead, we can talk about a legal system that engaged its environment and reacted to social change. Islamic formal legal norms and cultural norms stood not in opposition to each other, but to the contrary, they engaged and interacted with each other and thereby formed a legal system that can be described as Islamic as well as customary.[336] The wide range of actors influencing the legal process reflects this notion very well. Aside from jurists, we saw that the ruler, his diverse representatives, judges, muftis and even the common people played a bigger or lesser role in accounting for the evolution of Islamic law.

Of course, the role of jurists as interpreters of the Sharia and creators of *fiqh* cannot be downplayed. We came across examples where we saw that jurist authored works of the four schools of jurisprudence reached an almost code-like status, but we also encountered examples where the norms of *fiqh* were not followed to the letter. We have to be cautious to regard norms in *fiqh* books as laws proper or as "the Sharia". They are more likely to represent guidelines, especially in cases that do not fall into the strict category or worship and rituals (*taʿabbudiyyāt/ ʿibādāt*). If we add to that the fact that even under the regime of *taqlīd* the norms of *fiqh* were not resistant to change, then I would argue that jurists were guided by principles in their reasoning and law making. Ideally, behind every norm of *fiqh* there is supposed to be a concern, a purpose or a protected interest that is in the mind of the jurist, which he wants to protect and safeguard. Depending on time and space there are

---

[336] Fadel, "State and the Sharia," p. 97-98.

different means to achieve that. Furthermore, in their legal treatises jurists cannot cover every possible case, allowing them to list every possible scenario and the respective "means or measures" that have to be taken or chosen in order to safeguard and protect what is of concern.

Fiqh books of substantive law present us "the going opinion" of a particular *madhhab* during a given time and place. Aside from methodological factors these opinions often time come about through pragmatic considerations, and are also based on a prevalent social, cultural or economic context. Realities, which are prone to change and thus, the norms of *fiqh* do not constitute the last word on a certain subject.[337] More promising than the study of the norms, would be the study of the lawmaking process itself, in order to get a better understanding of the *fiqh* sphere of the Sharia. However, what are the limits of such a principled adaptation, especially if we consider cases where the foundational texts, Koran and Sunna, are very clear and only allow for one interpretation?

Additionally, the role of the state was important as well, be it in its function as final arbiter in cases of juristic disagreement, or in its prerogative to structure the law through administrative and procedural means, or in the rulers and his representatives' capacity as equal interpreters of the Sharia, such as jurists. We can say that Islamic scholars of the past agreed that the state is a necessary and legitimate element of the Islamic legal system, but they disagreed on the scope and the limits of his function. Some scholars conceded a bigger amount of discretion and authority to the ruler and others tried to constrain him through their procedures of *fiqh* as much as they could. This could be seen as a power struggle that depended on a lot of non-legal factors and the historical context, such as whether or not the ruler was secure in his reign, or whether his power was under threat and

---

[337] ʿAbd al-Raḥmān al-Jazīrī, *Islamic Jurisprudence According to the Four Sunni Schools*, trans. Nancy Roberts (Louisville: Fonts Vitae, 2009), p. xxxi-xxxii in the Introduction by Sherman Jackson.

weak, or whether he was at war etc. The ruler stood in a continuous power struggle with different elements of society, of which the scholars were only one among others, and the boundaries of the ruler's authority were always subject to an ongoing process of negotiation. Depending on those different factors the ruler was either only allowed to interfere in the process of lawmaking through certain procedural or administrative means, or at other times and places he was even allowed to have some legislative powers. Therefore, the question regarding who holds legitimate authority in lawmaking in Islam, should be seen primarily through the lens of "political power struggle", since the scriptural sources do neither privilege the state, nor the jurists, nor any other group or individual in this regard.

Meaning for Today

In most Middle Eastern Arab countries, the state managed to restrain the religious establishment by employing them as state servants. Usually those official scholars do not challenge the state's authority. Instead, we see that popular elements, such as "Islamists" try to claim "Islamic normativity" for themselves and challenge the state's authority, which they regard as "unislamic". The contemporary struggle between the state and "Islamists" in the Middle East could be seen in a similar vein as the power struggle between pre-modern states and the jurists. In that struggle notions of the Sharia play a very important role, as each side knows about the strength of the claim of "Islamic legitimacy".

This is one reason why some narratives of the Sharia can be problematic and why it could be useful to study the legal practice of pre-modern Muslim societies and the relationship between law, state, jurists and society. As Stilt says, "we actually have very little understanding of the historical experience of Islamic law, especially for the pre-

Ottoman period"[338], which allows Islamists to promote their own, often idealized, conceptions of an Islamic past as a normative model which one has to emulate.[339]

The narrative of the dominant historiography still informs and shapes our understanding of the legal reforms that occurred in the modern period in the Middle East during its encounter with the West. According to which modern Muslim states step by step replaced the Sharia with Western law codes, which is one among a number of reasons that led to the prevailing notion today that Islamic law is incompatible with the modern state, and therefore there is no Islamic law anymore.

This statement is only valid if we agree with the dominant historiographies understanding of Islamic law as a jurists' law, because in fact, the law codes introduced in the 19th century and afterwards differ considerably from the *fiqh* books, in terms of form, language, and content, in that they do not quote verses from the Koran or *aḥādīth* from the life of the Prophet. Moreover, those codes are not the product of *madrasa* educated jurists who arrived at laws through the application of for instance al-Shāfiʿī's legal methodology at scripture.

But, if we accept a broader definition of Islamic lawmaking and Sharia, by subsuming under Sharia the role of the state, legal practice and notions of equity and justice that are not explicitly mentioned in scripture, and even consider the notion that the *fiqh* of scholars is only one among several other legitimate interpretations and articulations of "Islamic normativity", then the picture changes fundamentally.

Such an understanding does not allow for a dichotomy between Islamic Law as a whole and modernity, because it acknowledges that the subject matter and the institutions of Islamic law changed over time and thus, are allowed to evolve. New narratives based

---

[338] Stilt, *Islamic Law in Action*, p. 4.
[339] Ibid.

around such a broader conception of Islamic normativity would reshape our views on so many topics that this would have a very serious impact on today's debates on the role of Islam in Muslim countries, the relationship between the secular modern state and Islam, reform of Islam and Islamic law, and further questions regarding the life of Muslims in non-Muslim countries, peaceful coexistence between Muslims and non-Muslims, the status of non-Muslim minorities in Muslim countries, human rights and Islam.